WILLFUL
INJUSTICE

WILLFUL INJUSTICE

A Post-O.J. Look at
Rodney King,
American Justice,
and Trial by Race

By Robert Deitz

Regnery Publishing, Inc.
Washington, D.C.

Library of Congress Cataloging-in-Publication Data

Deitz, Robert.
     Willful injustice : A post-O.J. look at Rodney King, American justice, and trial by race / by Robert Deitz.
          p.   cm.
     Includes bibliographical references and index.
     ISBN 0-89526-457-9
     1. Koon, Stacey C., 1950-   —Trials, litigation, etc. 2. Powell, Laurence—Trials, litigation, etc. 3. Trials (Police misconduct)--California—Los Angeles. 4. King, Rodney. 5. Fair trial--California—Los Angeles. 6. Los Angeles (Calif.)—Race relations.
I. Title.
KF224.K66D45   1996
363.2'3'092—dc20   95-52642
                                                           CIP

Published in the United States by
Regnery Publishing, Inc.
An Eagle Publishing Company
422 First Street, SE, Suite 300
Washington, DC 20003

Distributed to the trade by
National Book Network
4720-A Boston Way
Lanham, MD 20706

Printed on acid-free paper.
Manufactured in the United States of America.

10 9 8 7 6 5 4 3 2 1

Books are available in quantity for promotional or premium use. Write to Director of Special Sales, Regnery Publishing, Inc., 422 First Street, SE, Suite 300, Washington, DC 20003, for information on discounts and terms or call (202) 546-5005.

DEDICATION

This book is dedicated with admiration to two very strong people: Mary Koon, the wife of Stacey C. Koon, a woman who has kept both faith and family together during five years of almost intolerable stress, and my wife, Sharon Hott Deitz, whose encouragement and support have been as important to this book as the writing itself.

CONTENTS

ACKNOWLEDGMENTS

Alfred Regnery is, in my view, perhaps the most courageous book publisher in America today. Putting his reputation and even some measure of business profitability on the line, he has taken the lead in the public defense of a widely unpopular (in many quarters) but righteous case, the most politicized criminal case this nation has witnessed since the Sacco–Vanzetti trial of the early 1920s. Without Al Regnery's influence, it is doubtful that anything even remotely approaching the truth about the Rodney King episode would have ever been aired in any broad fashion. This book, like the one that preceded it, Sergeant Stacey Koon's *Presumed Guilty*, is a tribute to Al Regnery's belief in and commitment to the American system of justice.

In addition to Al, I am grateful to Trish Bozell for another fine job of editorial advice and counsel and to David Dortman at Regnery Publishing, who never complained when deadlines were stretched in midmanuscript by an aging computer that expired at an untimely moment.

Ira Salzman, the Los Angeles attorney who represented Sergeant Koon in the federal criminal and civil trials, provided invaluable aid, as did his persevering assistant, Kelly Sullivan. Thanks to both of you for allowing me to impose upon your time and knowledge.

Several current and former members of the Los Angeles Police Department (LAPD) generously shared their expertise. Prominent among them were retired Captain Robert Michael; Sergeant

Charlie Duke; Detective Susan Clemmer; and Patrolman Rolando Solano. As still-active members of the LAPD, Clemmer, Solano, and Duke deserve special recognition. By talking on the record about the Rodney King episode, they have exposed themselves to possible retaliation from the highly politicized LAPD management and command structure. I hope this won't happen; they are the kind of courageous cops we need on the streets today.

Retired Assistant Chief John Driscoll of the Dallas Police Department again provided expert and uninvolved advice on police procedures and policies. And, as usual, my agent, Evan Fogelman of Dallas, was helpful in all matters from helping to ease travel plans to encouraging me when the words weren't coming easily.

Former LAPD Patrolman Timothy Wind has suffered enormous personal and professional losses even though he was found innocent of any wrongdoing in the Rodney King episode by three consecutive juries. Tim Wind dispassionately and objectively shared information about what happened on March 3, 1991, and the impact of the Rodney King episode on his career, marriage, and health, although doing so doubtless was painful.

Federal prosecutors Steven Clymer and Barry Kowalski, although they were aware of my bias in this matter, were courteous in responding to telephone calls and providing, to the extent that they were able, their own perspectives on the case.

In addition, I am grateful for the assistance rendered by several other current and former members of the Los Angeles Police Department and other government agencies who provided information and documents that otherwise would not have been available. For obvious reasons these people must remain anonymous, but you know who you are.

Finally, any errors that appear in this book are wholly the responsibility of the author and no one else who assisted with the manuscript. Thanks to all of you.

AUTHOR'S INTRODUCTION

This is a book I did not wish to write. I was reluctant for two reasons.

First, I never actively sought to become involved in the Rodney King episode. I had viewed the infamous George Holliday videotape, repeatedly. Based on that superficial observation, I was convinced that the incident consisted of rogue Los Angeles police officers out on a mission to beat a black man whose only crime was his race and whose bad luck it was to have had a chance encounter with racist Los Angeles cops.

Initially, after seeing the videotape, I judged LAPD Sergeant Stacey Koon and Officers Laurence Powell, Theodore Briseno, and Timothy Wind to be representative of a fundamental malignancy of racism that had spread poison throughout American law enforcement.

The view was reinforced by personal experience. I had paid at least partial dues as a civil rights advocate and thus had a biased view of cops with racial attitudes.

Let me be specific: I had participated as a sympathetic reporter in the "long hot summer" of black voter registration in Mississippi in 1964.[1] During May and early June of that year, I became acquainted with Mickey Schwerner, Andrew Goodman, and James Chaney, the three civil rights workers murdered by racist cops and Klansmen that summer.

I had met the three civil rights activists on two occasions and respected them for their all-consuming, even religious commitment

1

to the cause of racial equality. In fact, I was supposed to accompany the three young men on that fateful trip on Sunday, June 21, 1964, when they left the COFO headquarters in a black neighborhood of Jackson, the state capital, to look into the recent destruction of a black church in nearby Philadelphia. I had spent the night of Saturday, June 20, in Grenada, about seventy-five miles north of Jackson, and on that Sunday morning was headed south to meet the three young men.

The only hitch that prevented my meeting them (and, presumably, an inconveniently premature burial beneath an earthen dam where the bodies of Schwerner, Chaney, and Goodman were hidden after brutal torture and ultimate execution) was a racist cop in Canton, Mississippi.

The cop, whose name I'll never forget but is unimportant to this story, had stopped me in Canton for violating traffic laws. My crime was driving a car with an out-of-state license plate. It was a seizure of body and property that I protested.

My protests were a mistake, a serious mistake. The officer and two other cops took me to the county jail, and there worked official intimidation on me for a couple of hours.

Among other things, they told me that they could protect me while in Canton, but if I got off the main highway onto a state road… well… and with this statement left hanging, the officer pointed through a window to the street outside, where three bib-overalled men wearing cowboy hats and carrying shotguns leaned against a pickup truck. They didn't look like the sort of people you'd include on your thank-you note list after a Sunday morning tour of the Madison County jail in Canton.

Still pointing at the men, one of the cops said, "I can't vouch for your safety outsida' town, boy, and not even in town if you're still here after dark." He then stressed, as if I hadn't gotten the point, "Do you understand what I'm sayin'?"

As a former U.S. Marine Corps infantry rifleman infused with an acute sensitivity to dangerous situations, I understood very well. Even so, the cops took another hour or so to explain in more graphic detail what might happen if I didn't hie my young body to Jackson immediately, without venturing off of U.S. 51 South. I had no difficulty obeying. But the couple of hours I spent in Canton were sufficient for Schwerner, Chaney, and Goodman to decide that I would not arrive in time to join them in their visit to Philadelphia where the church had been burned.

So the three young civil rights workers left without me. Their journey within eighteen hours, certainly no more than twenty-four, led to brutal torture and execution. To this day, I have been unable to watch the movie *Mississippi Burning* because of the fear it engenders, a reminder of how close I came to losing my life that day at the hands of racist cops with an ugly agenda.

And so it was in June 1992, when publisher Al Regnery called. I had never met Al Regnery, although I knew he was a publisher of reputable standing and I had read and admired some of his titles. He asked if I would be interested in helping to organize and write the cops' side of the story in the Rodney King incident. I immediately said, almost without thinking, "Not really."

But Al persisted. He wanted me to look at a rough collection of notes written by LAPD Sergeant Stacey Koon, whom I had described as "Sergeant Goon" to my former newspaper colleagues. I was repelled by the idea, despite my need for a cash infusion. While talking with Al, I wrote a sticky-note message and handed it to my wife. The note said: "He wants cops' side of the Rodney King story."

She vigorously shook her head, miming, "No, No, No!" On the phone with Al, I parroted her message, but more diplomatically.

Al said, "Wait a moment, let me send you the material overnight. Just look at it. And even then don't make a decision. I'll pay for a plane ticket to Los Angeles so you can meet with Stacey Koon and talk with him. Then you can decide."

That seemed fair, so I said OK, especially since Al had added as a deal-closer that he was also talking with another possible author. That casual statement recalled the depleted state of my bank account. So it was that on the morning after receiving Al's package, I sat down with the rough notes and disorganized material Stacey had written about the Rodney King arrest and began reading. I got to about page ten, looked up at my wife, and said: "These guys might be innocent."

The reason for this unsettling uncertainty was that, given my preconceived notions and the Holliday videotape, Stacey had written something that just didn't make sense to me at the time. He told about his reaction when he learned, the day after the Rodney King arrest, that a videotape had been made of the incident. His reaction was wholly unexpected.

"Great!" he had written. "Now we have an in-the-field tape of a live incident to show recruits at the police academy about the proper use of escalating force. How to take it up, how to take it down, depending on what the suspect does. That's the way the use of force works, and now we've got it on tape!"

That comment made me ponder: Why would a guilty person be pleased, even proud, to have a videotape, apparently irrefutable evidence, of his alleged crime?

For someone whose suspicions of racist cops had been forged in the crucible of the 1960s Southern civil rights movement, someone who had seen the Holliday videotape repeatedly and was convinced of the officers' wrongdoing, it was a defining moment. For the first time, I began to question whether my eyes had told me the truth, to wonder if eyes can deceive you when you don't know precisely what you're watching.

And so I agreed to take Al Regnery's plane ticket and visit Stacey Koon in Los Angeles. Stacey and his wife, Mary, met me at the airport. We got into his vehicle, and I told him politely that I wasn't convinced of his innocence and wasn't sure that I wanted to work on the book with him.

Stacey laughed. It was a nervous laugh, as I've learned the gesture sometimes to be. "Okay," he said. He explained that he lived in a Los Angeles suburb, about a forty-five–minute drive north of the Los Angeles airport. If he hadn't convinced me of his innocence by the time we got to his house, Stacey said, he'd turn right around and drive me back to the airport and I could return to Dallas and forget the whole deal.

It was a fair proposition, although it seemed loaded against working on the book. After all, three months before, during the trial in Simi Valley, it had taken Stacey hours on the witness stand to tell his story to a jury that had found him not guilty of wrongdoing. And now he was proposing to persuade me in forty-five minutes? Not likely, I thought.

Stacey began recounting what happened with Rodney King on March 3, 1991. He told the tale in rapid-fire fashion, dispassionately, the way a cop would report an incident in the field. By the time we got to the Golden State Freeway just north of the Van Nuys airport and barely halfway to his home, I had become more than just a partial believer. Four days later, after finishing an hours-long series of tape-recorded interviews and going over the videotape several times frame-by-frame and examining other documents, I was a committed believer.

And this leads to the second reason I didn't want to write this book. I never wished to write a sequel about Stacey Koon's life in prison, which is, of course, partially what this book is about. Because it is my firm conviction that he should never have been sent to prison, much less tried a second time, for a crime that wasn't a crime. Indeed, learning about his story, and assisting Stacey Koon with the first book, *Presumed Guilty,* was one of the most professionally important and spiritually enriching experiences of my life.

I am convinced that Stacey Koon is an innocent man, innocent not only of the specific charges leveled against him and his colleagues, but also of any prejudices that his critics clearly believed to have motivated his actions on March 3, 1991. He is a brave man, too, and a cop totally without racial prejudices that would intrude upon high standards of moral purpose. He was and is a good citizen, yet he has been brutally, even savagely, mistreated by the law enforcement and political establishments in Los Angeles, California, and Washington, D.C. However much I did not want to write a book about his conviction and imprisonment, I am proud to be part of his story even if it is only as a teller of his tale. And I am prouder still to call him a friend.

Throughout this book I have tried to be fair. But as you have doubtless surmised, this is not an objective account. Nor is it altogether complete, since the focus is on just two characters—Rodney King and Stacey Koon.

Many other people have suffered as a result of this episode. Begin with the three other officers who have endured three successive prosecutions as a consequence of the Rodney King episode—Laurence Powell, Timothy Wind, and Theodore Briseno. Then you must add the hundreds of people who had friends and family members killed or injured, their property lost forever in some cases, in the Los Angeles riots of late April 1992. There is no question that these people are victims as well.

Doubtless, too, people closely associated with Rodney King also have suffered. This group would certainly include King's family, and Bryant Allen, a passenger in King's car on March 3, 1991.

But the focus is on Stacey Koon, because he was in command of Powell, Wind, and Briseno that night. Koon has steadfastly insisted that he alone should be punished for any alleged wrongdoing. It was an unequivocal acceptance of command responsibility that is rare in today's world, certainly at the Los Angeles Police Department.

Rodney King is important, too, because he was the catalytic agent who created the events of March 3, 1991, and all that has transpired. If Rodney King had simply pulled over at the first flash of red lights in his rearview mirror, exited his vehicle, and obeyed legal police commands, the nation—and certainly the lives of hundreds of thousands of people—would be very different today.

Finally, the evidence presented in this book should create doubts about the fairness of our judicial system even for those people who believe the cops guilty of violating Rodney King's civil rights. For if you believe that Rodney King was maltreated by the officers, you must also conclude that the officers have suffered far more severe punishments than any alleged misdeeds warrant and that Rodney King has avoided any punishment at all for much more serious violations not of just the law but also of the boundaries of ordinary decent behavior.

And if, on the other hand, you believe as I do in the officers' innocence, what you will read in this book leads to an inescapable conclusion: Guiltless men have had their lives ruined for a grotesque purpose of cynical racial politics. Two men have been jailed for crimes they didn't commit, while government officials above them who consciously and deliberately blinded themselves to the truth have gone unpunished and in some cases even been rewarded for their treachery to the cause of justice.

The extent, moreover, of the damage done to our system of justice by subordinating truth to racial expediency cannot yet be fully calculated. We've already seen the bitter fruit of the Rodney King episode played out in the O.J. Simpson trial, when defense attorney Johnnie Cochran urged the jury to make its decision more on racial grounds than on the evidence. That was only Scene II of Act One; only a naïf would dare suggest that it will be the last, especially since the federal government itself set the pattern in the Rodney King episode.

Please read on. Let the evidence speak for itself.

ROBERT DEITZ
DALLAS, TEXAS
JANUARY 1996

I

EPILOGUE AS PROLOGUE

November 23, 1995, was Stacey Koon's forty-fifth birthday. It was also the day a gunman planned to kill him as revenge for being the supervising officer in the arrest of Rodney King on March 3, 1991.

Randall Craig Tolbert, an aging Riverside, California, gang member, had gotten drunk the night before, on Wednesday the twenty-second, and told family members he intended to kill Koon, who had been convicted in April 1993 for violating Rodney King's civil rights. Five weeks before Thanksgiving and his forty-fifth birthday, Koon had been released from the Sheridan, Oregon, federal correctional camp and sent to a halfway house at Rubidoux in Riverside County, California, about a hundred miles from his home in suburban Los Angeles.

At first, Koon was pleased with the assignment to Rubidoux to finish the supervised portion of his thirty-month term. Riverside County, he thought. That's not so bad. At least it's not as bad as South Central Los Angeles, where the 1992 riots followed his acquittal on state charges that were little different from the federal indictment. South Central LA would have been almost a death warrant for Koon; street rumor in South Central LA had it that gang members had put a $50,000 bounty out for anyone who would kill the former LAPD police sergeant.

What Koon didn't know was that the Rubidoux neighborhood where the halfway house was located wasn't much different from

9

South Central LA—a predominantly black and Hispanic area dominated if not controlled by street gangs.

Tolbert had been a gang member since his youth. He had a rap sheet to prove it—time in prison, charges of murder, robbery, assault on a police officer, assault with a deadly weapon, and numerous drug violations. Gang members flaunt rap sheets the way military heroes wear ribbons on their breasts as professional biography. But, at age thirty-four, Tolbert's image was lagging behind younger gang members who, still in their teens, were beginning to take power on the streets. Tolbert had to do something dramatic to regain respect. Like kill Stacey Koon. And the $50,000 bounty, if it wasn't just a rumor, wouldn't hurt, either.

So Tolbert decided to kill Koon. His family talked him out of trying to do it on Wednesday night. But Thursday morning was a different story. On Thanksgiving Day 1995, Tolbert made his mark on history.

But it didn't work out as Tolbert intended. Koon had a furlough for Thanksgiving and his birthday. He left the halfway house early that morning and went to his home and family.

Several hours later, about 11:00 A.M., Tolbert showed up at the halfway house. He was carrying a black plastic garbage bag. It contained some booze, a few drugs, chewing gum, and a weapon known on the streets as a "snake charmer."

The "snake charmer" is hardly a professional assassin's weapon of choice. It is basically a shotgun sawed off short enough to be legal, but it fires a .410 shotgun shell or comparably calibered lead slug. It is a single-shot weapon and called a "snake charmer" because it is used primarily to kill small animals, varmints, and vermin. The .410 shotgun pellets spread broadly to cover a wider area than a single bullet and thus make accuracy almost unnecessary. That works fine with snakes that drop out of trees into fishermen's boats in Texas, where the "snake charmer" was devised, but it's not intended for use on people.

Even so, it was Tolbert's weapon of choice. Or maybe it was the only weapon he had available. Whatever the reason, he invaded the Rubidoux halfway house shortly before noon on November 23, 1995, and demanded to see Stacey Koon. Told that Koon was on furlough and not on the premises, Tolbert demanded that Koon be called at home by telephone. With a weapon weaving in their faces, halfway house inmates and staff readily complied. Tolbert called Koon at home, shouting into the phone, "Get back down here, mother fucker, you fucking cop faggot, get your ass back here, I'm going to blow you away."

Koon immediately called the police to notify them of the hostage standoff that was going down. He talked with Tolbert a second time, then a third. Koon's cop instincts kicked in. By manipulating the conversation, he was able to learn where Tolbert was in the halfway house, how many hostages he held, the type of weapon he was using, what would be the best avenue of approach for a SWAT team now forming to rescue the hostages and end the situation. Koon is a professional; Tolbert wasn't.

In the meantime, Tolbert had gotten increasingly frustrated and violent because of his inability to find his target. He pistol-whipped one of the hostages, a Hispanic woman from the neighborhood. From a distance, he shot a twenty-two-year-old halfway house inmate in the chest; the shotgun pellets spread, doing no serious damage to the hostage who was able to escape. Another hostage, sixty-seven-year-old Karl Milam of Phoenix, Arizona, who was at the halfway house only to help a friend refill vending machines with candy and other snacks, wasn't so lucky. Because Koon had understandably declined to arrive for his own execution, Tolbert shot Milam in the head, killing him instantly.

About 3:30 P.M. the standoff ended. The Riverside County Sheriff's Department SWAT team broke through the front doorway. A cop stumbled over Milam's body at the same time Tolbert leaped from around the corner of a room and fired the snake charmer at the officers. The SWAT team's M-16 automatic rifles popped. Four magazines, each containing sixteen rounds of lethal ammunition, poured into Tolbert's body. He died on the spot.

In news stories the next day, the *Los Angeles Times* described how residents of the halfway house neighborhood in Rubidoux didn't want Koon assigned there in the first place. "It was like they were trying to slap us in the face by putting him [Koon] here," said Randall Tolbert's brother, Deric. The gangland assassin was described as a troubled man who was "putting his life back together" by starting a business to videotape weddings and such, and that on Thanksgiving

Day he had planned to bake a cake for his family never mind that family members said Randall Tolbert had been strung out on PCP (angel dust) and other, less powerful, drugs for at least three days before Thanksgiving.

Altogether, had the incident not ended so tragically both the event itself and the news media's handling of it would be almost high comedy. But it wasn't funny.

To the contrary. The attempt on Stacey Koon's life was an almost inevitable event, all but guaranteed by an atmosphere of racial revenge that had been established, condoned, and sustained by the federal government's prosecution of the Foothill Four officers and aided by the media's presentation of the March 3, 1991, arrest of Rodney King. What Randall Craig Tolbert attempted to do illegally is little more than what the government has sought to accomplish through legal means, however questionable the legality of those means might be.

And, finally, the worst part is this: The story is not yet over. It will continue to play out for as long as the government subordinates genuine justice for all citizens to political expediency and encourages more trials by race rather than truth, fairness, and the protection of personal liberties guaranteed by the Constitution of the United States.

II

A SOLOMONIC VERDICT: THE SECOND TRIAL

Over a forty-eight–hour period starting on Saturday, April 17, 1993, two seemingly unrelated events captured the attention of the nation. Even if unplanned, the two were almost coincidental and the timing of both was under the supervision if not outright control of the Justice Department of the United States.

The first, about 7:30 A.M. local time in Los Angeles on Saturday the 17th was the long-awaited, and in some official quarters greatly feared, verdict in the second trial of four Los Angeles police officers. The four cops had been tried on federal felony charges of violating Rodney King's civil rights in the early morning hours of March 3, 1991, in the Foothill Division of the Los Angeles Police Department.

That trial was the second that had resulted from an incident captured on tape by an amateur cameraman, George Holliday, and aired by Cable News Network on March 6, 1991. It soon became one of the most replayed events ever captured for history by a camera. It was shown more frequently than filmed records of the *Hindenburg* dirigible, the murder of accused presidential assassin Lee Harvey Oswald, the flaming destruction of the space shuttle *Challenger*. Indeed, the Holliday videotape even made it to the Royal Academy of Art in Paris in 1993 under sponsorship of the Whitney Museum,

13

which called it a "work of art," according to newsmagazine reports. In short, the Holliday videotape became indisputable, filmed evidence of police brutality against blacks in America.

But was it indisputable? Was it really proof?

Most people certainly interpreted the film as such. But many other people, whose voices were overwhelmed by opinion that was shaped largely by the constant replaying of the Holliday videotape, didn't see it as absolute proof of police racism. A lot of cops, and certainly many if not most who had experience on city streets that have become war zones, were able to see the Holliday videotape from a different perspective. To them, the tape reflected a regrettable but inescapable fact of modern life: Police work is sometimes brutal and violent. Most cops with street experience saw the incident for what it actually was—a potentially dangerous, unsearched felony evader, resisting arrest, and being taken into custody for obvious and witnessed violations of the California criminal code.

To many unthinking people, though, the videotape became a symbol of racism not only because it was aired so frequently, but also because it had been conveniently edited to eliminate the first few seconds that showed Rodney King either rising to escape or to assault Powell physically. Why the media edited the tape in such a fashion is unknown; one possibility could be that the portion showing a combative Rodney King didn't fit neatly into a slot labeled "police brutality." But why the tape was so edited is largely beside the point. The significant fact is that the crucial first four seconds of the Holliday videotape reveal an aggressive Rodney King whose intentions are not known by the officers, a felony suspect who has not yet been searched to determine whether he was armed.

Not until almost a year after the Simi Valley trial did network television for a brief period show the entire tape, including the critical first few seconds. It was the edited version that was aired literally thousands of times in the days after King's arrest and before and during the first state trial of the officers in Simi Valley in early 1992. It was shown hundreds of times between the acquittal verdict and the Los Angeles riots. It was aired during the riots, pouring volatile fuel on an already raging fire. It was shown before and after the officers' indictment on federal charges of violating Rodney King's civil rights and before, during, and after the federal criminal trial. It was shown as the two convicted officers were awaiting sentencing, after the penalties were imposed, and as they entered into federal custody. And each time the viewer saw the incomplete, consciously edited version.

The pace accelerated after the Simi Valley verdicts of not guilty were announced, and Los Angeles almost immediately erupted in a seething maelstrom of shooting, looting, burning, and random, senseless violence that left more than fifty people dead, hundreds seriously injured, seven thousand–plus arrested, and some $1 billion in property destroyed. In the days during and immediately after the riots, the three major networks alone broadcast the incomplete Holliday videotape a total of forty-six times collectively, according to Accuracy in Media. And this doesn't include the countless hundreds, perhaps thousands, of times the tape was aired by local television outlets nationwide. Thus the media, acting almost entirely on its own, convinced the public of the inevitability of rioting if, after the next trial, a federal court jury were to find the officers innocent.

This is an important point to understand in the context of the second trial: The great fear of all government officials, from the smallest precinct in Los Angeles to the White House executive offices in Washington, was that another jury might also find the officers innocent. Because such a finding could—inevitably would, in the pack opinion of most media observers—spark another devastating riot. And the great fear was that this time, it wouldn't be confined just to Los Angeles. That view certainly prevailed in minority communities. According to all polls, most African Americans regarded both the King arrest and the first verdict in Simi Valley as irrefutable evidence of official police racism in America. Now a second round of riots in Los Angeles and maybe even other cities was openly predicted by some militant black leaders. And the media couldn't resist the temptation to presage new violence.

As early as August 17, 1992, hardly two weeks after indictments against the officers had been handed up by a federal grand jury, and long before a final trial date had even been set, *U.S. News & World Report* observed that "Few would discount the potential for new rioting in case of acquittal." And that sort of media speculation would grow to almost hysterical proportions as the subsequent trial drew near an end.

Federal Judge John G. Davies did everything within his power to keep a lid on the explosive powder keg. An Australian who had won an Olympic gold medal for his native country in the 1952 swimming competition, Judge Davies emigrated to the United States and earned degrees from the University of Michigan and the UCLA School of Law. After almost twenty-five years as a high-profile entertainment lawyer in Los Angeles, Davies was appointed to the federal bench in 1986 by then-President Ronald Reagan. Judge Davies ran a tight courtroom according to rigid rules, one that both prosecutors and defense lawyers praised as strict but fair. He made key decisions with an even hand that revealed no hint of favoritism. When defense lawyers objected to introducing harmful videotaped testimony from the Simi Valley trial, Judge Davies ruled against the officers with clear, logical reasoning. When prosecutors manipulated prior grand jury testimony by quoting it out of context, Judge Davies landed heavily on the U.S. attorneys and told them to cut out the nonsense and play by the rules.

One telling incident occurred at the end of the trial, as the jury left the courtroom on April 10 to begin deliberations. Sergeant Koon handed Judge Davies' court clerk a sealed envelope, but asked that it be given to the judge only after the jury had announced its verdict. Once Koon had been found guilty on one count—of failing to safeguard Rodney King's constitutional right to protection while in official custody—the judge opened the note. It said, simply and to the point: "Your honor, out of deference to your penchant for precise and succinct language; thank you for a *fair* trial" (emphasis added).

But despite Judge Davies' best efforts to keep the lid on tight, tensions built rapidly as the case went to trial, evidence was heard, closing arguments were made, and jury deliberations finally commenced. Much of the responsibility for the community's raw, inflamed nerves belongs with the media, which had turned the event into a circus of speculation. It was a preview of what would happen later with the O.J. Simpson trial. The enormity of that spectacle was probably avoided only because Judge Davies would not permit television cameras in his courtroom.

Outside was a different matter, though. In the plaza fronting the Edward T. Roybal Federal Building in downtown Los Angeles, television crews from around the world, manning twenty-five separate camera and satellite-dish installations, dominated the open space that had been sealed off with concrete barricades. It seemed that anyone with anything to say even remotely connected to the trial could wrangle fifteen seconds of sound-bite fame. According to the *Los Angeles Times,* the trial was covered by media representatives from fifteen nations, including Holland, Italy, Germany, Japan, France, and even Estonia. In a preview of the O.J. Simpson display, print reporters were falling over themselves in pursuit of stories, people to interview. Not all of the reporting was sensational. Indeed, some newspapers took pains to put the affair in some greater, more meaningful context. The *Los Angeles Times,* for example, solemnly told readers that Stanford University, the University of Southern California, and UCLA had reacted responsibly to the minority community outrage over the Rodney King incident by establishing sociology courses about the importance of the affair and what it meant for American life today.

Even so, when real news wasn't readily available, the *Los Angeles Times, New York Times,* and other prestigious publications fabricated "mood of LA" stories, almost every piece suggesting if not outright predicting violence in the event of an innocent verdict. Among other rumors dutifully reported by the press was one that twenty thousand armed gang members were prepared to launch a paramilitary assault on Los Angeles' prosperous western neighborhoods in the event of an acquittal. On balance, it was not the sort of journalism that eased anxiety in either prosperous white or minority environs.

As the jury retired to consider a verdict, some of the reporters' employers issued their troops protective gear—helmets, bullet-resistant vests, and such—in case of an innocent verdict and immediate rioting right outside the courtroom doors. Given the high fever of media speculation and *angst* in newsrooms, it's hardly surprising that the city's temperature rose in tandem.

Even before the announcement on Friday, April 16, that a decision had been reached, Los Angeles City Councilman Joel Wachs called for a dawn-to-dusk curfew and an early deployment of National Guard troops. "We cannot afford to wait for trouble to break," Wachs told the *Los Angeles Times.* "We have to send a clear and unambiguous message." Wachs was promptly and sharply criticized by a political rival, California State Assemblyman Richard Katz, who said Wachs' comments violated the line separating "demagogu-ery from decency." Katz accused Wachs of "trying to tap into the people's basic fear and exploit it to the nth degree," according to the *Los Angeles Times*. Wachs and Katz were running for office at the time, and, indeed, the trial falling right into the middle of munici-pal election campaigns in Los Angeles did not soothe the festering wound Los Angeles had become.

No one would dispute that fears were there for exploitation. Con-sider the disposition of Los Angeles when the case went to the jury for deliberation. The Los Angeles Convention and Visitors' Bureau said it had surveyed hotels to make sure sufficient rooms were avail-able for riot police and military personnel if a sustained martial deployment became necessary. City officials openly discussed plans to delay municipal elections planned for April 20. Before the ver-dict was rendered in the second trial, some corporate executives in Los Angeles publicly announced the existence of their contingency plans for evacuating employees from downtown locations in the event of post-trial violence. Roman Catholic Cardinal Roger M. Mahony of Los Angeles publicly urged that the verdict be delayed until after spring break for schools, when the streets would be filled with stu-dents of all ages.

Newspapers and television broadcasts reported that the federal government had given special riot-control training to a battalion of eight hundred U.S. Marines at nearby Camp Pendleton outside of San Diego, close enough to be rushed into the city if needed. More than six hundred California National Guardsmen from the 160th Mechanized Infantry Regiment had been activated and moved to the city, along with four armored personnel vehicles to protect sol-diers in a "high-threat environment," the California National Guard told newspapers.

City Councilman Nate Holden asked that the verdict be read in early morning, say 3:00 A.M., when potential troublemakers would have difficulty rounding up a crowd they could stir into a frenzy of violence. The Los Angeles County Sheriff's Department was on twelve-hour, seven-day shifts, and every deputy on twenty-four–hour call. The Los Angeles Police Department, with a new chief at the helm following Daryl Gates' resignation under pressure after allega-tions of a too-slow response in the 1992 riots, had made its plans for instant reaction, too; thousands of LAPD officers who worked the streets had received refresher training in riot control within the past year. A question occurs here: If the LAPD believed the officers were guilty, then why should they be so concerned about another verdict of innocence that they would spend time and money preparing for another riot? The answer is obvious: The LAPD command structure knew very well that the officers' case was solid.

But let's move on from the background to April 19, 1993, for a brief look at the second Justice Department–controlled event, which came within forty-eight hours of the verdict in Los Angeles.

As the palpable tension blanketing Los Angeles and occupying the nation was beginning to subside, early in the morning of April 19, 1993, Federal Bureau of Investigation agents launched a military raid complete with helicopters, armored vehicles, and chemical weapons on the Branch Davidian compound near Waco in central Texas. The Branch Davidians were an obscure but armed, dangerous, and besieged religious cult that had held out for fifty-one days after an abortive raid by federal law enforcement officers failed to produce a voluntary and peaceful surrender. The initial raid was necessary, the government said, because of charges that the cult and its messianic leader, David Koresh, had violated laws regulating possession of illegal firearms.

And what was the relationship between these diverse events, one in Los Angeles and the other in Waco?

If perhaps subtle, it is still difficult to ignore. No one knew how the trial in Los Angeles would play out. No one knew if a diversion of national attention might not be needed to avert another riot and further bloodshed and destruction. The jury had announced on the afternoon of April 16, 1993, that it had reached a verdict. But both the city of Los Angeles and the federal government had urged that the verdict be withheld to permit law enforcement agencies to get riot control personnel in place. Thus Judge Davies kept the jury sequestered and delayed announcing the verdict until Saturday morning, April 17.

Perhaps there was not even a casual relationship between the timing of the Branch Davidian raid and the verdict in Los Angeles. Former Federal Judge William Sessions, whose tenure as head of the FBI spanned both the Rodney King episode and the Branch

Davidian incident, said he would be "astounded, shocked, and amazed if there were any relationship between the two events."[1]

Yet another curiosity: The original raid of the Branch Davidian stronghold occurred on February 28, 1993, as the federal trial was just about to begin. Granted that the original raid was conducted by the Treasury Department's Alcohol, Tobacco and Firearms Division, the ATF, not the Justice Department's FBI. Still, this February 28 assault followed the World Trade Center bombing in New York City by only forty-eight hours, once again grabbing headlines away from a negative news event over which the government had no control.

Granted that two instances of coincidental events do not add up to proof of a link or government conspiracy to manipulate events as a way of controlling headlines and public attention. But as any police detective will tell you, at some point multiple coincidences establish a pattern that can appear powerfully suspicious even if quite innocently unrelated.

For example, consider the viewpoints expressed by retired Captain Robert Michaels of the Los Angeles Police Department. Michaels is an expert in paramilitary operations and SWAT tactics and strategies. For more than twenty years, he taught not just police officers but also FBI agents and military personnel how to train for, plan, and execute special operations. He is, in short, an expert's expert. And he says mounting a raid as complicated as the one at Waco required something more complex than simply pushing a button. He believes it is unlikely the Justice Department decided to launch the raid *after* the verdict was announced, *after* tensions had started to ease. More likely, he says, a decision to push the "execute" button came as the trial drew to a close and a verdict, possibly of innocence, was imminent.[2] And, indeed, that timing was confirmed during congressional hearings in July 1995 on the Waco incident, when the Justice Department acknowledged that the decision to raid the Branch Davidians probably was made on April 16 or April 17— the time span during which the verdict was reached, delayed, and then announced.

Michaels, it must be noted, is not a disinterested observer. He testified on the officers' behalf during the first trial in Simi Valley. He did so voluntarily, although he had never met any of the defendants before the state criminal proceedings. Michaels offered strong support for Koon's contention that the officers operated well within the guidelines of LAPD policies and procedures governing appropriate uses of force, and he was outraged by the LAPD command structure's failure to support its officers.

Michaels' outrage was fed by the subsequent federal prosecution that resulted in a criminal conviction, and he used the Branch Davidian incident as a springboard to appeal to Attorney General Janet Reno's sense of justice, since Reno had said she assumed "full responsibility" for the meltdown outside of Waco on April 19, 1993.[3]

In a May 26, 1993, letter to Reno, Michaels wrote:

> I am impressed with your assumption of responsibility for the actions of the federal officers which brought about the Waco, Texas, conflagration.... There is, unfortunately, a glaring absence of this type of courage by most people in today's striving for political correctness.
>
> I have waited a month in hopes that your example might stir the many politically correct people who bear responsibility for the police actions in the [Rodney] King matter and that they would come forward and assume their responsibility. I am not completely surprised but am still saddened that *not one* single person responsible for police administration, supervision or legal interpretation of training in the use of force within the City of Los Angeles has come forward to speak truthfully and assume responsibility for the conduct of the officers in the King matter [emphasis in the original].

Michaels told Reno in his letter that as a former LAPD commander and training officer, he was willing to offer himself up for prosecution in connection with the Rodney King episode. Then the former street cop, SWAT trainer, and LAPD commander put the matter in clear focus for the nation's chief law enforcement officer:

> Use of force is not an exact science, but the principles are clear, and the actions employed by the officers in the King matter were consistent with those principles long ago established and still in place. *The force may be disgusting,*

*distasteful or revolting and no longer acceptable in our society,
but that is not within the officers' means to determine or control.*
Their conduct was within the guidelines set forth by duly
constituted Los Angeles leaders at the time the force was
applied on March 3, 1991. To even charge the officers is to
change the law after the fact. That which was acceptable
and legal before the fact, and had been for years, became
illegal after the fact and so we have *ex post facto* judicial
determination of criminal activity.[4] This is unfair, morally
wrong, and should be unconstitutional [emphasis
added].

Reno never responded to Michaels' letter.

The hypocrisy of the Justice Department in hounding police
officers toward a prison term while letting its own officials off
the hook for an astonishingly more deadly use of force was bad
enough, Michaels said.[5] But it was compounded, in his experienced view, because "there was absolutely no urgency" in launch-
ing the raid on April 19. "That [standoff near Waco] had been
neutralized," he said. "There was no need [for the FBI] to go in
at the time they did."[6]

No need, of course, except perhaps official worries about what
might happen in Los Angeles and what newspaper headlines and
TV news broadcasts might say if the four officers were acquitted a
second time and another round of riots erupted. And so, even if
merely coincidental, even if the government didn't burn the village
to save the city, to paraphrase a memorable bit of cynicism from the
Vietnam War about government policies, the timing of the two incidents couldn't have been better—at least theoretically. But even if
the Waco raid didn't go as the FBI had scripted and ultimately became
a public relations nightmare in itself, it nonetheless almost completely
overshadowed the Los Angeles verdict in the national media.

What could have been a public relations disaster for the Justice
Department—an innocent verdict for all four officers and a new
outbreak of violence—suddenly became stale news because of Waco.
And what actually happened—two officers found guilty, two innocent—was hailed by the government as a victory and was then quickly
dismissed.

This occurred even though the split decision was barely acceptable to minority leaders as an unsatisfying compromise. But the protests of minority leaders got almost no attention. The raid on Waco had guaranteed that they wouldn't. The flames at the Branch Davidian compound blotted out minority leaders' criticisms of the verdict. More important, television broadcasters reduced disapproving remarks to sound bites against visual photographs of the 1992 Los Angeles riots that bore an eerie resemblance to the smoking ashes near Waco that by now dominated prime-time newscasts.

In short, in the brief, forty-hour news cycle (thirty-six hours for television) between the LA verdict and the Branch Davidian horror, dissident minority voices got little media attention.

A comment by then-Mayor David Dinkins of New York City was pushed back to page 34 of the *New York Times* on April 18, the day after the verdict was announced. "I thought all four [officers] were guilty," Dinkins said. "We must accept the verdict. That doesn't mean I have to like it." Brooklyn Hispanic leader Luis Garden Acosta, chief executive of *El Puente,* a community organization, focused on the two acquittals. "I believe the two individuals found not guilty represented the millions of Americans who in the face of injustice turned the other way," Acosta told the *New York Times.*

In South Central Los Angeles, when the verdict was announced, a weeping Reverend Jesse Jackson told congregants at the First African-American Methodist Episcopal Church, "We have been given a reprieve by this jury. This is neither justice nor Armageddon" Benjamin Chavez, the new executive director of the NAACP (since deposed), said, "The state failed us last year [in the Simi Valley trial]. The federal courts have only partially served us…. We will not have a false celebration for partial justice." Detroit Mayor Coleman Young called the verdict "a weak, belated response to what was an atrocious beating." None got much attention from the media.

To the contrary, this time around the media put on a happy face by emphasizing pleased official reaction and downplaying the dissatisfaction with a Solomonic verdict that carried out its threat to slice the baby in half.

On page 1 of the Sunday, April 18, *New York Times,* the subhead beneath the main story was: "Tension Eases As Residents Hail the Verdict." A page 1 subhead in the *Los Angeles Times* on

Sunday reported that "Los Angeles wakes up to a day of anxiety and rejoicing."

The ensuing story in the *New York Times* reported that "many residents of this tense city greeted the convictions... with cheers, while the police, on full mobilization with riot gear, relaxed their guard."[7] In Los Angeles, a sidebar to the main *Los Angeles Times* story painted Los Angeles in bright, almost festive, holiday colors. It was as though Jack the Ripper had just been nabbed and once-terrifying Los Angeles streets were again as safe as a babe snuggled to its mother's nurturing bosom. "This battered city seemed to open and brighten just after 7:00 A.M. when it was announced that two of the four officers had been found guilty," the *Los Angeles Times* said. "Traffic moved smoothly amid a general feeling that the split verdict had brought at least half a measure of justice."

Of course, not everyone was happy with the convictions of the two officers, but these reactions got virtually no attention except occasional sound bites from Koon's and Powell's separate defense lawyers, whose graveyard reaction could be expected. Sure, a few grousing LAPD street cops were interviewed by the media. But these officers had to be careful about what they said in public; the Rodney King episode had forcefully demonstrated how LAPD management could extract revenge on street cops who embarrassed the department or otherwise didn't march neatly in lockstep with company policy. Characteristic of these officers' guarded responses was one quoted in the April 18 *New York Times*: "Now maybe we can get back to work," the officer grumbled after the verdict was announced.

Not that there wasn't a lot of support for Koon and Powell. There was. But no one in the media apparently bothered to search for people who might find the verdict at odds with truth, reality, and justice. Or if the media did look for such people and found them, their voices were muted.

You see, plenty of ordinary citizens went out of their way to let the court and attorneys know how they felt. In the weeks between the jury verdict and sentencing, literally thousands of letters supporting Koon and Powell filled the mailboxes of the two officers and their attorneys. Lawyers in Philadelphia, Phoenix, Seattle, Colorado, and Florida wrote to offer advice on grounds for appeal of the guilty verdicts. A Mill Valley, California, attorney wrote to suggest how to get the most favorable prison accommodations. A legal briefing business in Southern California offered free services for appellate work. Even a Japanese law professor in Tokyo sent Ira Salzman, Koon's attorney, copies of pro-cop legal articles he had written—the reprints were in the original Japanese.

At El Camino College in Torrance, California, retired LAPD Lt. Frank D. Wissman, professor emeritus of administration of justice, wrote to Judge Davies, "Are we going to add further sorrow to this human tragedy we have witnessed in this case by making these officers [Koon and Powell] scapegoats to the community and the media? Every police officer identifies with these two men.... 'There but for the grace of God, go I' has been quoted many times in the [police] locker rooms and roll-call rooms."

After the guilty verdict but before sentencing, Sandi Martinello of Los Angeles wrote the U.S. Probation Office protesting the fact that the officers had been tried at all. "Jurors have publicly stated that they dismissed expert testimony [during the trial] and 'relied solely on the [Holliday] tape.' God! Then what was the purpose of the 'trial'? What kind of justice system is that? What more does the public want? Perhaps to make an example of them? The last pound of flesh? Do we keep trying police officers until we get a guilty verdict? We all know they were tried twice for the same acts."

In a newsletter to clients, Greg Meyer, a law enforcement consultant in Bellflower, California (and also, not coincidentally, a lieutenant on the LAPD), advised police officers subscribing to his service: "The beating of Rodney King was a predictable tragedy. Its roots are found in a series of poor public policy decisions which occurred nine years before the King incident. Thus far, the wrong people have been held accountable.... We must wonder why the decision makers who created the policies which allowed (even encouraged) officers to beat people with metal pipes were not themselves on trial as co-principals who aided, abetted, advised, and encouraged Sergeant Koon and Officers Powell, Wind, Briseno, and thousands of other LAPD officers."

That's a central, critical point, the same one raised by Michaels in his letter to Attorney General Reno: Why were the foot soldiers prosecuted, while the generals who gave the commands let off the hook? It seemed to reverse the Nuremberg trials, where the field marshals got hanged first for giving orders; the troopers, who merely followed those orders, were punished later but only rarely handed over to the hangman for extreme cases of criminal activity. Indeed, at one point Judge Davies even asked questions suggesting to Koon's attorney, Ira Salzman, that Davies believed the wrong people were being tried.

But the question of ultimate responsibility for the policies that led to the Rodney King episode was almost entirely missed by virtually all of the national media that had stirred up such a frenzy about the affair. Televised news accounts of the Rodney King story hardly even mentioned police policies, procedures, and training as a reason for the incident, even though this was a cornerstone of the successful defense laid out for the Simi Valley jury.

According to an analysis of 123 network news stories about the Rodney King episode done by the Center for Media and Public Affairs, police training and instruction were cited as a cause for the violent arrest only five times; Rodney King's refusal to obey legal police commands as a reason for his beating was mentioned in four of these reports. In contrast, general police brutality was stated forty-one times. Clearly, the root causes for the incident were largely ignored, while the incomplete Holliday videotape was overwhelmingly influential in molding opinion, facts notwithstanding.

With the verdict in and Waco on fire, now was the time for the media to wrap all of this up in a neat little package. Thus when the federal trial verdicts came down on April 17, prominence was given to a statement by Barry Kowalski, a self-described liberal Democrat and Carter administration civil service career appointee to the Civil Rights Division of the Justice Department in Washington. Kowalski had spent the better part of a year in Los Angeles preparing for the trial, formulating strategies, and then directing the government's grand jury investigation and subsequent presentation of the government's case in court. "I think a year ago [after the Simi Valley acquittal of the officers] the conscience of the community, the conscience of the nation, cried out for justice, and this verdict provides justice," Kowalski said.

California Governor Pete Wilson, a Republican, said simply, "Justice has been done." A deputy chief of the Los Angeles Police

Department, although presumably acquainted with departmental policies and procedures that cast doubt on the guilty verdicts, parroted the company line: "Justice has spoken." Attorney General Janet Reno asserted that "justice has prevailed" and promised that the Justice Department was "going to do everything it can to continue to bring prosecutions to ensure that the civil rights of all citizens across the country are protected." Former Attorney General William P. Barr, who got the federal prosecution steamroller moving in the closing days of the Bush administration, said the verdict "vindicates the judgment we made to proceed with the case…. I think justice was done."

President Clinton, in Findlay Township, Pennsylvania, pulled out all the stops as he announced the verdict to an early morning crowd on April 17: "This verdict was a tribute to the work and judgment of the jury and the efforts of the federal government in putting the case together," the president said. "And it did establish what a lot of people have felt in their hearts for two years: That the civil rights of Rodney King were violated.

"But I ask you to think about the deeper meaning of this whole issue," President Clinton continued. Then, in a breathless leap of logic to elevate what should have been a routine felony arrest to majestic, even hallowed, proportions, the president explained that "deeper meaning": "Surely the lasting legacy of the Rodney King trial ought to be… a determination to reaffirm our common humanity and to make it a strength of our diversity."

Never mind that Rodney King was not on trial despite overwhelming evidence of a felony offense, something the president should have known. And never mind the obscurity of how the jury decision "reaffirmed our common humanity" or the "strength of our diversity." These, after all, are moral concepts that have thus far in human history eluded the best spiritual efforts of Jesus Christ, Yahweh, Buddha, Allah, Vishna, and a host of trifling secular almighties, not to mention sociopolitical systems ranging from Athenian democracy to Brazilian rain-forest tribes who devour their neighbors. It is unlikely in modern America that a jury in such a highly politicized trial could reach such noble objectives. It didn't matter. The thing was done.

Yes, the Los Angeles jury had apparently been up to the task of affirming the Bush/Clinton-style of justice. Of course, the twelve jurors had some help in reaching the politically acceptable decision.

Maybe President Clinton, Attorney General Reno, Governor Wilson, and the editors of the major daily newspapers and newsmagazines didn't know what that assistance was. But other people were in on the squalid little secret. Those in the information loop about how the government had ruthlessly abused its power, and the defendants and their lawyers, included Kowalski and his lead trial assistant, Steven D. Clymer from the Los Angeles U.S. Attorney's office, along with the top managers of the Los Angeles Police Department. These people knew very well the tools that had been used to get a guilty finding. And what were those helping hands?

The main ones were perjury, misleading and incomplete testimony, and witness intimidation, all of which are described in detail later in this book, and all were condoned and encouraged by the federal government. And these were just the three big ones. To these you can add the prosecution's withholding of evidence from the defense because that evidence supported the defendants' contention of innocence. Which offense is, of course, in violation of federal rules of evidence. Nor does this short list include probable juror misconduct, which was a fault of the panel and not of the prosecution or defense.

But here perhaps is the worst part of all: All of these offenses rolled along in an even-handed, bipartisan fashion. Both Republicans and Democrats were in on the fix, as were senior officials of the LAPD, and past and present members of the Los Angeles City Council. These were people who either knew—or should have known, in the post-Watergate parlance of the media—what was going on.

And let's not forget the probable silent partners, such as many of the reporters of the trials, and their editors, who did not tell their readers—either deliberately or through casual neglect—about evidence or developments that might pierce the cloak of nobility surrounding Rodney King and the Justice Department prosecution. They offered instead a steady diet of self-righteous effusions about racial equality and civil rights, however little if anything these had to do with the Rodney King episode.

The inescapable conclusion is that justice was the last thing the local, state, or federal governments, not to mention the media establishment, wanted in Los Angeles. What they wanted were convictions and nothing less. Only convictions would satisfy the roaring beast of racial politics. Only convictions could prevent another riot.

The media establishment wanted convictions, too, but for different reasons. Although another riot would make a good story, a second finding of innocence could raise embarrassing questions about how the media had presented the entire Rodney King episode to the public.

And so the government and everybody else in the clamoring mob got the convictions they wanted, at least partially. It was hardly justice, of course, because the wrong people went to jail for crimes they didn't commit. But, then, justice never was the goal in the federal criminal prosecution of Koon et al. A basic lesson here is this: When the federal government and the media, with all of the awesome powers these institutions possess and use, want to get you— you're going to be gotten.

That's where the Branch Davidian raid really paid its public relations dividends. By the time people had an opportunity to examine the Los Angeles trial in more detail and maybe start asking troubling questions, the media and their government handlers were off and running with the Waco story. So, by April 19, 1993, most ordinary Americans sighed with relief that the Rodney King affair was apparently over, turned their attention to Waco, and got on with their lives.

Most people, that is, except for Stacey Koon and his colleagues, and Rodney King and his attorneys. They still had more trials and ordeals to face. The government hadn't even started to work on Koon and Powell. Nor was the Los Angeles Police Department through with Wind and Briseno, even though they had twice been found innocent. Subsequent events would suggest that the objective was not just to punish Koon and Powell, but to destroy them altogether.

And why did the establishment want them destroyed? The answers are simple. To the LAPD command structure and the city's political establishment, Koon and Powell were throwaway items that could be casually discarded so no damage could be done to the reputations of senior police officials and politicians who wrote the policies that led to the Rodney King episode. And the government's payoff was even more direct: Of what use was justice for four street cops when their sacrifice could satisfy the raging passions of racial politics?

It is more of a tribute to the human spirit than to the U.S. legal system that the government has been largely disappointed in its goal—to finish off a single individual. Maybe it was because he'd learned to live with deadly peril during almost fifteen years of patrolling the most dangerous streets in Los Angeles. Or perhaps it was simply his religious faith.

Whatever the reason, Stacey Koon wasn't going to roll over and play dead for the government just because other people had lied, distorted the truth, and danced across the lines of legal behavior. These people apparently had gotten away with such behavior, while the street cops were left holding the bag. But the story wasn't over. In fact, the story wasn't even half begun.

III

MATTERS OF CHARACTER

I have a dream that my four little children will one day
live in a nation where they will not be judged by the
color of their skin but by the content of their character.

The Reverend Dr. Martin Luther King, Jr.
August 28, 1963

The Third Trial

If the federal court jury hearing the case against the Foothill Four police officers had used the noble criteria etched in memory by the Reverend Dr. Martin Luther King, Jr., few logical thinkers possessing all of the facts about the Rodney King episode would dispute this proposition: Sergeant Stacey Koon would have gone back to policing the streets of Los Angeles, and Rodney King would have been hustled back to prison for admitted parole violations.

31

But, of course, Dr. King was an idealist and not an attorney, certainly not a government attorney. Character is a subjective and arguable concept. It has little if anything to do with the administration of laws.

Courts and juries deal with facts, evidence, and law. Who did what to whom, and where, when, why, and how are the cogent issues that emerge in a criminal trial. That a defendant may attend church faithfully, give regularly to charity, or is unfailingly kind to animals is largely unimportant in a criminal trial. In the courtroom, character usually doesn't arise until after a defendant has been judged guilty and punishment is under consideration. Even then, depending upon the jurisdiction or a judge's whim, matters of character aren't always allowed into the record.

This is important. It makes the trial records of the Rodney King episode all the more significant, since character was not a principal topic of jury consideration.

You see, one fact has been lost on many people: Koon, Powell, Wind, and Briseno have been tried not twice but three times for the Rodney King incident, and the cops have won two of the three trials even though character was not considered by two of the three juries.[1] Those three trials were the state proceedings in Simi Valley, the federal criminal trial in Los Angeles, and King's civil suit against the officers.

At the state trial in Simi Valley, Rodney King did not testify and LA County prosecutors carefully avoided any discussion of character. The purpose behind concealing King from the jury was to prevent any reference to his prior run-ins with the law for offenses ranging from robbery to spousal abuse to solicitation of prostitution. Revealing that sort of information to the jury could have been highly embarrassing for two reasons.

First, it would have buttressed the defense contention that Rodney King was a violent, uncontrolled, unsearched, aggressive felony evader the night of March 3, 1991. The fact is that by March 3, 1991, at age twenty-five, Rodney King had accumulated a rap sheet that was beginning to look as unsightly as used thrift-store underwear. That pesky little truth wouldn't have helped the prosecution's argument that King was a helpless victim brutalized by savage cops. Or, as the *Los Angeles Times* characterized King more than once, "a cowering black motorist," a description that casually ignored the clear evidence that he was neither cowering nor a mere motorist. Rodney King was a felony evader who used his considerable physical strength—he's about six feet, four inches tall, and weighs more than 220 pounds—to resist arrest in the early morning hours of March 3, 1991. And the Holliday videotape—even the cut version—proves that fact.

Second, and maybe even worse for the prosecution in a world where perceptions seem to be more important than reality, raising King's qualities of character in open court would have provided the defense with an opportunity to contrast King's background with Koon's on-the-record character. It would have given the jury a chance to weigh the relative reliability of testimony from a convicted felon, accused wife-beater, and patron of prostitutes against the squeaky clean record of Stacey Koon.

That's a contest King couldn't have won. Koon is an active church member with no criminal record; partner in a durable marriage of twenty-plus years; attentive father of five children; and holder of a bachelor's degree in criminal justice and two master's degrees, one in criminal justice and the other in public administration, all earned while on full-time active duty as a Los Angeles street cop. At the time of the Rodney King arrest, Koon had a fourteen-year record of conduct marked by some one hundred commendations for meritorious service, including the LAPD's second-highest award for personal bravery, and another for giving mouth-to-mouth resuscitation to a black male prostitute—a suspected and later-proved AIDS sufferer—who had collapsed unconscious while in Koon's presence as a supervisor.[2] These factors far outweighed the three disciplinary notations in his "jacket," or personnel file, for relatively minor matters, none of which involved racist attitudes or illegal use of force.[3]

This is not to say Koon is a saint. He's human, just like everyone else. But he isn't a police party animal of the type described by Joseph Wambaugh in his books (*The Blue Knight, The New Centurions,* etc.) about the LAPD. Koon largely avoided socializing with his colleagues. He preferred social activities centered around family and church. He drank only occasionally, perhaps two six-packs of beer a month. On balance, Koon is a solid citizen. Imagination is beggared by the proposition that Rodney King could have come out ahead or even tied Koon in a contest about character at the Simi Valley trial.

King did testify at the federal criminal trial, but character and past behavior didn't become a major issue. And King did acknowledge that he was on parole from the California Department of Corrections the night of March 3, 1991, and that he fled from police to avoid being returned to prison for violating conditions of his release after serving not quite half of a two-year sentence for robbery.

King said he sought to outrun four high-powered police cruisers with his four-cylinder 1988 Hyundai Excel because "I was kind of hoping the problem would go away by ignoring it.... I was scared of going back to jail."

Such reasoning might have been illogical, even absurdly so considering the array of police officers pursuing him that night. Yet it was hardly a damning admission to put before the jury; running from cops to avoid going back to the cooler provided an understandable, if hardly commendable or even sensible, motive for King's behavior that night.

King also acknowledged under cross-examination at the federal trial that he lied when it was to his benefit to do so. This admission came in response to questions about the several different, often conflicting versions of the incident that he had given to authorities at separate times in the months since March 3, 1991.

Again, though, while lying in one's own interests may not be estimable conduct, it is not uncommon. Lying for one's own benefit is a familiar human frailty, and Rodney King cannot be judged as wicked for doing what most politicians do as a matter of routine job performance. So it's doubtful that many, if any, of the jurors were shocked by King's admission that he lies on occasion.

Only in the third jury trial, King's civil suit seeking at least $15 million in damages from the four officers, did comparative character, morality, and social responsibility emerge more fully for jury consideration. Only in the third trial did jurors learn additional details about the past history of King's drug usage, spousal abuse, petty crimes, and felony offenses. Each of these drew a sharp contrast with Koon's record of family responsibility, professional achievement, and commitment to civic duty through a career in law enforcement marred only by his recent conviction in the second trial of violating Rodney King's civil rights.

And this matter of character almost certainly influenced the third trial's racially mixed jury, which was composed of three white men, three white women, and one Filipino American, one African American, and one Hispanic, all women. It was the same panel that had awarded King $3.8 million in an earlier suit against the city of Los Angeles.[4]

Given the racial mix of the jury panel that heard both cases and given that the city had already been found liable for damages, a reasonable person could assume that the officers would have to cough up money, too.

But the jury voted against awarding King one single penny in damages. True, the jurors dutifully determined that the officers "had acted in reckless disregard of Mr. King's constitutional rights." But since that finding had already been made by the federal criminal jury, it would have been difficult if not impossible for the civil panel to say otherwise.[5] That the jury decided anyway that King didn't deserve any damages was significant—and not because it seemed to contradict the ruling that King's civil rights had been violated or because it prevented future claims on any money the cops might earn.

It was important because it meant that in subsequent proceedings King would be unable to collect ransom from the cops to pay his attorneys' fees that already were exceeding $1 million. In order to collect that money, King would have to be considered the "prevailing party" in the civil lawsuit against the officers. And, as Judge Davies wrote, the fact that the jury awarded him $0 in damages meant that "Mr. King cannot be considered the prevailing party."

In other words, the cops won. As one juror told the *Los Angeles Times* immediately after the trial ended in June 1994, "There was no doubt in my mind that Mr. King was at fault for a good deal of what had happened. The police officers were using the tools they had been given."

Nor was there any doubt in the mind of King's attorney about who won the civil trial. King attorney Milton Grimes complained to reporters after the civil trial, "Goddamn it, we got robbed!" Grimes continued, "I don't think we can say this is the final chapter in the trilogy of Rodney King.... We're still looking for justice."

One can only wonder whether Grimes was talking about the fact that King won no damages against the officers or whether he was concerned about not being able to collect lawyer fees from the cops.

Subsequent events suggest it was more the latter than the former, especially since Grimes was fired by King after the federal civil trial failure and replaced by Steven Lerman, who had been King's initial attorney of record. Whereupon Grimes sued his former client, Rodney King, in July 1995 for more than $1 million in legal fees Grimes said were still outstanding as a result of an oral agreement he had made with King. Lerman disputed Grimes's claim. Earlier, Lerman and Grimes had squabbled for more than two years over who would represent Rodney King and cash in on the meal ticket each apparently believed Rodney King to be. Lerman and Grimes filed charges against each other with the California Bar Association, where the dispute ultimately limped into oblivion.

Character: The issue surfaces throughout the Rodney King episode. And the point here is that even if usually inadmissible as evidence in court, matters of character are central to understanding the entire scope of the Rodney King episode.

Character: A casual contempt for the law and civilized behavior under rules all citizens are expected to obey guided Rodney King's actions in the early morning hours of March 3, 1991.

Character: Obedience to orders and LAPD training, policies, and procedures governed Koon's response to Rodney King's conduct.

Character: Allegiance to justice and not political expedience should be fundamental to democratic government, which makes the Justice Department's vendetta against Koon, Powell, Wind, and Briseno ignoble and unexplainable except in the context of racial politics.

Koon's and King's contrasting records of character and behavior before, during, and after the incident in the early morning hours of March 3, 1991, clearly suggest that neither the federal government nor Los Angeles officialdom sought justice.

If underlying character—one small example being that King repeatedly changed his story and lied, while Koon's version of the event has been wholly consistent from the beginning—as an explanation of behavior had been important to the investigation, federal officials never would have sought an indictment, much less taken the case to trial, manipulated a guilty verdict through legally questionable means, and then sought the most punitive penalties possible.

In the end, what the Los Angeles political and police establishments and the federal government wanted was not justice. The objective was to identify scapegoats to sacrifice on the altar of racial politics to prevent another riot.

In short, the government made its judgment on the basis of skin color and not the content of character, in blunt rejection of the ideals of the Reverend Dr. Martin Luther King, Jr.

Stacey Koon, Laurence Powell, Timothy Wind, and Theodore Briseno are white. White people wouldn't riot in the event of a guilty verdict. Rodney King is black and had become a useful symbol for power-seeking minority leaders who had loudly warned that black people would again take to the streets if the officers weren't found guilty.

The government's response couldn't have been more clear: Racial politics governed the government.

And so: To hell with matters of character, to hell with justice, to hell with the Reverend Dr. Martin Luther King, Jr.'s idealistic view that character is more important than skin color.

Sergeant Stacey Koon

In a moment of whimsy shortly after entering the Federal Correctional facility at Camp Parks in Dublin, California, in October 1993, Stacey Koon described the first few days in prison simply as an adaptation of his prior experience in law enforcement.

He and Laurence Powell were involved in "a new type of policing," Koon wrote to a friend. "Policing for cigarette butts. You'll be happy to know we were top producers. In fact, they (the BOP—Bureau of Prisons) must have known we'd do a good job because they gave us a Cadillac the first day. A Cadillac is one of those little metal trash cans with a handle and a short broom.[6] You've seen them at Disneyland, Magic Mountain, etc. Yes, it's a comfort to know the BOP has given me OJT (on the job training) for a successful [post-prison] career."

Occasional drollery in letters and phone calls to friends was a defense mechanism Koon developed to maintain spirit and optimism during his twenty-four months in prison from October 13, 1993, to October 16, 1995, when he was transferred to a Southern California halfway house to prepare for eventual complete supervised release under terms of the thirty-month sentence imposed by Judge John G. Davies. (The thirty-month sentence was appealed by the government as too lenient, and the Ninth U.S. Court of Appeals agreed with the federal prosecutors, ordering the case back to Judge Davies for more severe punishment. Then Koon won a Supreme Court hearing on that ruling. But all of this will be discussed in greater detail in a later chapter.)

Wry wit may not have been the best psychological shield raised by Koon nor the most appropriate when dealing with generally humorless BOP functionaries. But humor, spiritual faith, the support of family, friends, colleagues, and thousands of strangers who wrote hundreds of sympathetic and supportive letters each month while he was in prison, were among the few tools available to sustain Koon's psychological health during his months in prison—these, and an unshakable belief in his ultimate vindication by the judicial system.

But however accepting he seemed to be outwardly, it must have been a major emotional ordeal to be on the inside looking out rather than vice versa, transformed by the judicial process from Sergeant Stacey Koon, LAPD, serial number 21667,[7] to federal inmate number 99752012 in the custody of the U.S. Bureau of Prisons. Too obviously, unlike Rodney King, Koon cannot be considered good raw material for the penal system. No, imprisonment was doubly hard for Stacey Koon, just as it would be for most people never convicted and put in lengthy custody as punishment.

For one thing, he is a devoted family man. One of the reasons he preferred working night shifts on the LAPD (usually 11:00 P.M. to 7:00 A.M.) was that it permitted him time with his children, whose ages were fifteen, thirteen, eight (twins), and six when he entered prison. "Mr. Mom" is what he called himself—father by day, cop by night, with vacations, days off, afternoons, and early evenings devoted to family activities.

Then, of course, there was the matter of having been a police officer for almost fifteen years. Police officers have problems in prison. For one thing, cops are accustomed to authority. Koon, as a former police field supervisor, is especially so attuned. From the first, Koon's goal was to acquire experience on the streets and then rise to a command position that would offer a street-cop balance to the political dominance of the LAPD management structure. He was an officer who enjoyed wisely using his authority, a cop who once said, after facing down and subduing a suspect in a confrontation that might have ended in gunfire, "I love it when command presence works." But those days are past, and whatever authority Koon had as a street cop is no longer part of his life.

The two federal correctional camps where he was imprisoned follow a regimen that is not very different from being on a relaxed military post.

Like all other prisoners, Koon's activities were restricted and routinely monitored. Visitors were limited to specific hours for people on a list that required advance BOP approval. All visitations, except with attorneys, were monitored by a guard, with no note-taking, cameras, or tape recorders allowed. Telephone calls—outgoing only, no incoming calls authorized—could be made only to people on a BOP-sanctioned list, and calls were monitored or tape recorded. Visitation areas were confined to a single building and within a red-lined perimeter. Vending machines were off-limits to prisoners, since prisoners were not permitted to possess money.

And, too, there was the natural concern for physical safety. Because of the Rodney King incident, Koon's face was one of the most familiar in the Los Angeles area, and his name was known nationwide.

An InfoTrac information retrieval search of six newspapers with national influence revealed that 142 separate articles were published about Stacey C. Koon between March 3, 1991, and October 13, 1993, when he entered prison.[8] That's an average of about one every five days for thirty consecutive months. This doesn't include articles in *Time, Newsweek, U.S. News & World Report,* and other national magazines,[9] television and radio exposure, or the countless thousands of other media outlets across the nation.

To put this coverage in perspective, 142 articles on the InfoTrac system thrust a reluctant Stacey Koon into the major leagues of media exposure along with such publicity-hungry entertainers as Michael Jackson (52 major newspaper articles during a period when he was being accused of moral misconduct with children) and Madonna (31 stories at a time when she was promoting a soft-core porn photo book featuring herself in various sorts of gender-indifferent adventures).

The enormous amount of superstar publicity accorded Koon posed potential risk for his physical safety. Any cop sent to prison hazards retribution from other inmates, who see police officers as a natural enemy—an easy target when placed on equal footing with other prisoners.

For Koon and Powell, the risk was geometrically increased because of the Holliday videotape and its endless repetition, the intense media coverage of the Simi Valley trial, the riots that followed, and the federal government's subsequent prosecution. Judge Davies took note of this potential danger in his sentencing memorandum, when he wrote: "The widespread publicity and emotional outrage which have surrounded this case from the outset, in addition to the defendants' status as police officers, lead the Court to find that Koon and Powell are particularly likely to be targets of abuse during their incarceration."

That didn't happen. Koon says that when he first entered prison he was subjected to minor verbal abuse but nothing serious. Sometimes he'd pass a cluster of other inmates and hear one or more of them mutter something like, "He doesn't look so tough now, without his gun and club," or other derisive, at times more menacing, comments. He says he could have responded by confronting them physically and settling the matter outright. But to do so would invite attention from prison authorities—a negative goal he studiously avoided—and probably official punishment. After a while, when it became evident that he couldn't be provoked, the verbal assaults dwindled, although they never died. And, as the Thanksgiving Day 1995 incident at the Rubidoux halfway house vividly demonstrated, his post-prison life continues to be threatened.

The enormous amount of publicity accorded to Koon before he reported to the Dublin, California, correctional camp near San Francisco for confinement in October 1993 is one reason why he was placed in a category called "Central Inmate Monitoring" (CIM) by the Bureau of Prisons. Like any bureaucracy, the BOP does everything possible to avoid media attention. Unlike other federal agencies, the BOP rarely distributes press releases. By the very nature of its business, a penal system is nourished by secrecy and tormented by publicity. This does not imply anything sinister; an open-door policy is not consistent with the entire idea of penal confinement. Jails aren't built, nor are people put inside them, for public amusement.

This is one reason why the CIM category of confinement was established. Most routine BOP paperwork involving a specific inmate asks whether the prisoner has been the subject of publicity. In Koon's case, the "yes" box was checked with the terse handwritten notation: "Intensive."

Originally intended primarily as means of protecting inmates who had testified against mob bosses, today the category mostly means that a CIM inmate is simply watched a lot more closely than other prisoners. Koon was a CIM, along with a handful of other high-profile inmates.[10] In Koon's case, it had both good and bad consequences.

On the one hand, for example, CIM status meant that when Koon was transported between prison facilities, he didn't go by prison bus. Instead, he traveled by automobile, comfortably chauffeured, perhaps shackled in the back seat, with two U.S. marshal guards in the front. But the privileges were far outweighed by the disadvantages.

For example, as a CIM, Koon wasn't allowed the furlough privileges or conjugal visitation privileges accorded to most of the other inmates of the work camp. Ordinarily, an inmate with a record of good conduct is allowed supervised furloughs as the end of a sentence draws near, starting with twelve hours of unsupervised release and gradually increasing to encompass entire weekends and five-day workweeks. This privilege is intended to ease the prisoner's reentry into society.

Although Koon had served almost half of his sentence in the summer of 1994 when his father died, he was not allowed to attend his father's funeral unless accompanied by guards—whose salaries Koon would have to pay while under their supervision. Since prisoners are not allowed to have money and Koon's financial resources had been exhausted by the legal costs of his trials and appeals—more than $250,000 in all, not counting living expenses for his family since he was not drawing a paycheck from the LAPD nor of course earning any money while in custody—it was a Catch-22 situation. As a result, Koon could not attend his father's funeral.

CIM liabilities also surfaced when Koon was withdrawn from the work camp and put into an isolation cell in Los Angeles to testify in the civil trial, trial three, that resulted when King sought damages from Koon and the other officers. Although Koon testified only three days, he spent a total of fifty-six days in a seven- by nine-foot protective custody cell and was allowed to shower only once every three days.

News reports made slighting reference to Koon's appearance in court, dressed as he was in blue-denim prison garb, white socks, and sandals. Powell, also a CIM prisoner but with jailers who were more lenient, wore a business suit. The contrast was striking. Koon's problem was that the navy blue suit his wife had brought him to wear didn't fit because he had lost so much weight,[11] and prison guards wouldn't allow him to wear a belt, presumably out of concern that he might hang himself. Nor could Koon wear black socks, apparently because he might then be mistaken for a guard and make a daring escape from the courtroom. So he was left with no option but to wear prison clothing.

A more serious problem Koon encountered as a federal inmate came in 1995, when the Bureau of Prisons reclassified the Dublin correctional facility near San Francisco as an all-women's camp. Accordingly, Dublin's male prisoners had to be transferred to other institutions.

The Bureau of Prisons decided to move Koon and Powell to the Boron Correctional Work Camp near Edwards Air Force Base, only about one hundred miles northeast of Koon's home in the Los Angeles suburbs. Powell accepted the transfer, but Koon refused even though it would make family visits much more convenient.

The problem, Koon told BOP officials, was simply that Boron was a general population prison and it was too close to Los Angeles. Among other things, this meant that Boron housed not just white-collar offenders, but inmates of all types. And many of these were from South Central Los Angeles, where the 1992 riots had been most furious. Some of these inmates may have been imprisoned for nonviolent crimes, such as money laundering or tax fraud. But these convictions tended to be in connection with drug-related activities, which meant they probably came from a criminal underclass that might retaliate violently against the police officer blamed for the Rodney King episode and subsequent LA riots. Put simply, Koon's physical safety would be in great jeopardy if he were thrust into the general population at Boron with its high percentage of LA-area inmates.

So Koon gave a flat no to the BOP. To put him in Boron would require chains, dragging, kicking, and screaming. And that meant publicity, which the Bureau of Prisons didn't want. But then again they couldn't let inmates decide where they'd do time, either. Some punishment was necessary.

Accordingly, Koon was placed in isolation in the hospital prison ward at the Kern County jail in Bakersfield, California, while BOP officials decided where to send him for the remainder of his sentence. Koon says that if isolation was punishment, he could have used more of it. He had the leisure time to read and write, without the irritation of unwanted companions. He even gained weight during his eleven days in isolation punishment.

The Bureau of Prisons finally decided upon the Federal Correctional Work Camp at Sheridan, Oregon. So, in January 1995, Koon was taken out of the Kern County jail and driven to Sheridan, where he remained until his discharge to enter the Rubidoux halfway house on October 16, 1995.

Sheridan is a small farming community of about twenty-five hundred people in the heart of the Willamette Valley, about sixty-five miles southwest of Portland. It is a serenely beautiful, grape-growing, wine-making country. Thousands of acres of clover fields sustain a thriving dairy industry, and stately orchards of apple and pear trees line the roadsides. To the north and west, rolling hills gently rise to become the coastal mountain range, its peaks usually obscured by clouds.

The Federal Correctional complex sits atop a knoll overlooking Sheridan and this breathtakingly beautiful panorama. While the Federal Correctional Work Camp, where Koon and some five hundred other inmates were assigned, appears mild enough, a visitor quickly notices the concrete walls with razor-wire toppings at the nearby Federal Detention Center and Federal Correctional Institute, the next two higher levels of federal punishment.[12]

At Sheridan, Koon settled into the routine he had established at Dublin, a lifestyle treadmill intended to do his time one minute at a time, one hour at a time, one day at a time.

He would awaken about six o'clock each morning. Eat breakfast. Walk for exercise, usually about five miles a day. Then perform morning chores, using the "Cadillac" to clean the area around the one-story cinder-block visitor reception building of cigarette butts and other trash. (At Dublin, Koon worked the trash detail only briefly; his permanent assignment was as a clean-up orderly in the bath and restroom areas.) He did his job twice a day, and was paid $5.25 a month. Assuming that his job took about two hours each day, his pay came to about nine cents an hour.

After morning cleanup, he'd have free time to read, answer correspondence, write, make telephone calls, and attend to other personal matters. After lunch, he'd duplicate the morning routine. Then dinner and a free period until bedtime. Head counts or bed checks would be conducted six times daily—at midnight, 3:00 A.M., 5:00 A.M., 8:00 A.M., noon, 4:00 P.M., and 9:15 P.M.. A local priest visited the work camp each Saturday to say Mass (the priest reserved Sundays for his own parishioners), and Koon usually attended unless he had visitors, a regular if not frequent occurrence, considering the one thousand miles separating him from his family.

Although there are no razor-wire barricades, federal work camps aren't the leisurely "Club Feds" critics have made them out to be. True, some facilities have swimming pools, golf courses, tennis courts, and other amenities. But these civilities are confined to correctional facilities that once were military properties and subsequently transferred to the Bureau of Prisons. Which means, of course, that the leisure-time accommodations were already in existence and not constructed for inmates' amusement.

Sheridan is not a former military base and has no such diversions. The only exception is a running track used for exercise and some weight equipment for muscular development. Granted, a commissary offers inmates such apparent luxuries as smoked oysters and Fig Newtons, along with more ordinary goods like soft drinks, instant soup mixes, underwear, socks, and sneakers. But these items can be purchased only with money earned while in prison. And you can't buy many luxuries on $5.25 a month.[13]

From the beginning of his confinement, Koon was determined to generate positive consequences from a negative turn in his life. The routine he established stressed exercise, sensible dietary control, contemplation, and study. His weight, which had ballooned to about 215 pounds around the time of the federal trial because of physical inactivity, fell to a more normal level of 175. His walk did not lose its characteristic bounce, a stride some reporters had characterized as "arrogant," and his sense of humor remained intact.

Though he describes himself as suffering from post-traumatic stress from the overall ordeal of the Rodney King episode, he now looks upon the matter as having probably saved his life.

"I was pushing it to the edge of the envelope," he said in an interview while imprisoned at Sheridan. "Every New Year's Eve some drunk partygoers would get on top of some hotel and shoot off their guns, and every New Year's Eve I'd go up there and arrest them, knowing that some day my luck would run out and I'd get shot by some guy with a shotgun. But I'd still go up there every New Year's Eve, knowing that the risk got greater each time. It was almost like a soldier returning to combat, as if he wanted to get killed. All of that ended on March 3, 1991, and it probably saved me from getting hurt or killed someday."

While in custody, Koon sought to improve his condition in other ways, too. For one thing, he continued to study. He completed two in a series of Catholic Home Study mail courses in church catechism for future lay teachers. He has thought about writing, teaching, and other intellectual pursuits once the legal ordeal is finally ended.

Koon also has spent hours reevaluating the entire Rodney King episode. To do otherwise would be unnatural, since it has been such a defining moment in his life. And Koon has not wavered in his firm belief that he and his officers behaved properly in taking Rodney King into custody. "Remorse" is not a word in Koon's vocabulary when he talks about the Rodney King episode. He is, however, embarrassed at having become a symbol of martyrdom to many other police officers who see the incident as the most extreme example yet of an anti-law enforcement bias among politicians. But Koon acknowledges that the role couldn't have been avoided, simply because of the publicity the Rodney King arrest generated, if for no other reason.

He professes to have no overall bitterness but admits to lingering anger toward the Los Angeles Police Department command structure that he says (and evidence persuasively supports the proposition) hung him, Powell, Wind, and Briseno out to dry as sacrificial offerings on the altar of racial politics.

More pointedly, he retains harsh feelings toward former LAPD Chief Daryl Gates, former Deputy Chief Robert Vernon, and the LAPD command structure that concealed the truth about the department's training, policies, and procedures, all of whom scurried for cover when the Holliday videotape crashed down on the community.

As for Rodney King, Koon expresses an objective and even somewhat sympathetic viewpoint. Koon believes King was manipulated by racially inspired politicians and by King's own lawyers, in much the same way Koon and his officers were manipulated and wronged by their employers and the political system. Koon says he wishes King had "played his cards right" and "taken advantage of the opportunities" provided by the incident, specifically by using the $3.8 million windfall settlement from the city of Los Angeles to get educational or vocational training and break the cycle of reckless conduct that has marked Rodney King's adult life.

But that hasn't happened, Koon observes, and King continues to follow the same patterns as before the March 3, 1991, arrest. With Rodney King, Koon says, "there's a propensity to drink, there's a propensity to drive, there's a propensity to get arrested for that. There's a propensity to use drugs, a propensity to get caught. There's a propensity to pick up whores and get caught. There's a propensity to get in domestic disputes and beat up on his wife. It's just a repeated history. It's like a loop that's going around and around and around. That's exactly what's happened in Rodney King's case, and that's exactly what's going to continue to happen. He's not doing anything to break that chain, that syndrome. He's just caught in this loop, and he's going to continue to do what he's always done."

Koon says all of this about Rodney King with neither sympathy nor condemnation. His tone is objective, not angry. It is a street cop's cool, uninvolved, and rational analysis of perceived reality.

Rodney Glenn King

For one fleeting instant in his life, it appeared that Rodney King might be able to break the cycle of self-inflicted trouble with the law that had marked his past. (Rodney King would not meet with the author of this book as the manuscript was being researched and prepared. Nor would King's lawyer, Steven Lerman, allow himself or his client to be interviewed.[14] Accordingly, all information about Rodney King is derived from published reports and court records and other official documents.)

For one brief pause in an adult life characterized by an escalating series of accusations of one petty crime after another, finally leading to conviction for a serious offense that put him in prison, it seemed that the events of March 3, 1991, might be reshaping Rodney King's approach to life in a highly positive fashion.

That moment came as the Los Angeles riots reached a furious peak on May 1, 1992. As flames and smoke billowed over South Central LA, as hospital emergency rooms overflowed with injured people, Rodney King, dressed neatly in dark slacks, a white shirt, tie, and blue cardigan sweater, was brought before the cameras and microphones of a hastily arranged news conference. Present were more than one hundred reporters and television camera crews. Media representatives had difficulty hearing King's words, as police and emergency medical helicopters sliced noisily through the air overhead.

Videotaped accounts of the news conference show King saying, in a faltering tone fraught with sincerity, humbly and almost shyly, "People… I just want to say… you know… can't we… Can't we stop making it horrible for the older people and the kids? Can't we all get along?"

It was a quiet voice of reason and sanity in a community out on an insane rampage. As *Newsweek* magazine commented in its issue of May 9, 1992, "The stammered appeal quickly transformed King into a voice for calm and racial justice." *Newsweek's* judgment mirrored most other media reaction. In the span of a few brief seconds, Rodney King had become a reasonable voice pleading for compassion and racial reconciliation, a gentle giant brutally savaged by rogue cops and not a hulking monster threatening community safety. It was a remarkable transformation.

More to the point of character, it was almost a genuine and sincere entreaty. Sincerity and genuineness are difficult if not impossible to prove, but evidence supports the proposition that Rodney King's "Can't we all get along?" plea was a heartfelt message.

That usually elusive evidence was unwittingly supplied by King's own lawyer at the time, Steven Lerman, in billing memoranda submitted to the U.S. District Court in support of Lerman's request that the city of Los Angeles pay him more than $250,000 in fees and cough up an additional $100,000 in out-of-pocket expenses incurred to represent King.[15] Lerman had carefully scripted King's comments for the press conference. But the script didn't include the "Can't we all get along?" appeal, which was ad-libbed by Rodney King. In his billing memorandum for May 1, 1992, Lerman wrote:

"Concerned about use of videotapes [of] King's plea as *evidence of his dysfunction*. At this time, analyzed 'Can [*sic*] we all get along' speech to show how *King's mental process is disrupted*" (emphasis added). Lerman says this entry referred to the effect of the beating on King's neurological ability to reason and was not intended as a criticism of his client's having deviated from the prepared script.

Maybe so. But this wasn't the only time Lerman revealed casual disdain, at times even contempt, for his client, Rodney King, in billing memoranda. That, and an opportunity for Lerman to hit the big time as a civil rights lawyer in what might prove to be the most important anti-cop case on record, one that surpassed even the O.J. Simpson defense criticisms of the LAPD in terms of legal issues raised.

Lerman recognized this from the very first day he represented Rodney King as an attorney of record. But for Rodney King to pay off for Steven Lerman, his case had to be presented on television and in the newspapers, not in the courtroom.

On March 6, 1991, three days after the incident, Lerman's billing diary recorded: "Office is insane.... King case all over the media. I took every single call I could from various media's representatives, gave six interviews to different TV stations.... Immediately apparent his case will be [tried] in the media, at least until principles [*sic*] have their day in court.... Met with King to advise him of how I intend to portray his case in the media."

Two days later, Lerman saw his role as one of memorable, lasting importance. Lerman's billing notes said he was "highly charged by [the] opportunity to participate in [a case] that promises to be of historic proportions."

Lerman was a watchdog for King and wasn't above patting himself on the back for the good media job he was doing for his client—and making damned sure his client knew about it. "Many reporters have advised me that my undertaking to talk to them is, indeed, the proper way to handle the avalanche of interviews, as ignoring any one of them could result in a negative spin these [might] put on the King case," Lerman wrote in his billing diary for March 13, 1991.

But Lerman was also worried about the annoying problems posed by King's rap sheet. The record of offenses was tough to explain under the best of circumstances, much less in the glare of constant media attention. "Media now frustrated [with] reluctance to allow Rodney King to be interviewed," Lerman wrote in his billing notes for March 18. "Media now digging up King's past in an attempt to look for some interesting reading, i.e., 'smear' material, indicating the need for 'King's story' from him."

Then Lerman went on record with a Pontius Pilate act, washing his hands of any damaging publicity that might accrue if he didn't control his client. "Won't be responsible for the spin that may develop," Lerman wrote, if King met independently with the media.

But the *Los Angeles Times* came to Lerman's rescue on July 7, 1991. His memorandum for that day indicated that either Lerman was duping his client about the attorney's ability to control what went into newspapers or the media had become completely co-opted at this point. Either argument can be supported. Lerman's billing memo said: "Advised by Lois Timik [Timnick] of *LA Times*.... 'Will hold presses for Steven Lerman if further reaction to the story [develops].'" And Lerman wanted King to know that the attorney controlled the on-off button at the *Los Angeles Times'* presses, regardless of whether that was true. The memorandum added that Lerman "relate[d] comments [by *Los Angeles Times* reporter Timnick] to King as evidence of our ability to manipulate the media."

That comment should make the *Los Angeles Times*, or any other newspaper that prides itself on independence, experience at least a twinge of discomfort. Not many editors would relish knowing that a trial lawyer feels comfortable enough of "our ability to manipulate the media" to put the comment in print for the court record.

Nor should King feel entirely comfortable with Lerman's assessments of his client's conduct. On one occasion, according to Lerman's billing memoranda, the attorney said, in so many words, that King was a pain in the ass. On July 18, 1991, Lerman said he met with his client to review medical records, adding that "talk[s] with King must demonstrate great resolve, King can wear anybody out." Lerman contends this referred to the entire ordeal and not to King being a difficult client.

Again, maybe so. But overall, Lerman's billing records indicate a preoccupation with media relations that had equal, perhaps more important, weight as motivation to provide legal services to Rodney King. Judge Davies took note of this in his order drastically reducing the fees both Lerman and Grimes sought from the city of Los Angeles for representing King.

"Mr. King's lawyers," Judge Davies wrote, "and Mr. Lerman especially, basked in the friendly glow of media attention not for the purpose of obtaining a favorable result for Mr. King, but for their own benefit. It is inconceivable that the jury verdicts [in the civil suits] were related even in the remotest fashion to appearances by lawyers on talk shows or by the media spin of Mr. King's trial lawyers."

Grimes, too, got his hand slapped by Judge Davies for such peccadilloes as billing more than $1,000 in fees to attend the premier of the movie *Malcolm X* in Oakland, where King was a special guest, and another $1,000-plus to attend an Alabama A&M University event that featured a guest appearance by Rodney King. Grimes's bills, Judge Davies wrote, revealed "an excessive number of hours claimed in light of the services described," adding that Grimes's notations for several seventeen- and eighteen-hour days devoted exclusively to Rodney King were "implausible." These and many other bills Grimes—and Lerman, too—submitted were disallowed by Judge Davies.

But let's get back to the May 1, 1992, press conference at the height of the LA riots, when King made his famous "Can't we all get along?" comment.

It is curious that King's own lawyer would regard the statement as evidence of King's "dysfunction" and of how King's "mental process is disrupted." Surely the attorney should be rejoicing that his destined winning lottery ticket, a man characterized by police officers as "The Hulk," had been magically transformed by his own words and a willing media into a respectable resident of Mr. Rogers' cardigan-sweatered neighborhood, as *Newsweek* characterized King's performance at the press conference.

But, then, maybe Lerman was more on target than he intended. Maybe King's improvised statement *was* a dysfunctional act. Maybe it *was* a disruption of King's mental process. Because the plea for responsible citizenship displayed by Rodney King in front of TV cameras and print reporters on May 1, 1992, was aberrational, an isolated event in the public record of his contacts with society at large before, during, and after the predawn hours of March 3, 1991.

Rodney Glenn King was born April 2, 1965, in Sacramento. The family moved to Southern California while King was still an infant. It was a working-class family. His father and grandfather did odd jobs in construction and the like, and as a child Rodney King often helped them. The King family was extended, with about twenty-five cousins, aunts, uncles, and other relatives all living within two miles of each other in Altadena, a section of Pasadena where the family settled.

King's family called him by his middle name, "Glenn," originally spelled with double "n"s but shortened to "Glen" by later police reports that eventually became official records. Not until the incident on March 3, 1991, when his name became associated with racial victimization and police brutality, did he become "Rodney."[16]

King's childhood was unremarkable. He enjoyed sports, especially baseball, and played every position except pitcher and catcher while attending John Muir High School in Pasadena before dropping out in the eleventh grade. Homework and grades held little appeal for King. He was a slow learner and often avoided schoolwork in favor of playing ball. Even special education classes didn't help much because King had few intellectual tools to employ. According to California Department of Corrections records, at age twenty-five King had a tested intelligence quotient of 86, indicating slight retardation, and the average reading vocabulary, comprehension level, and mathematical skills of a third grader.

When he was about twelve years old, King made a good friend who would weave in and out of his life, a boy named Bryant Allen. Allen, whose nickname is "Pooh," became a close friend of King's, playing ball with Rodney, watching baseball games and nature documentaries on television (another favorite of King's), and sharing other wholesome boyhood activities.

But not all of those activities were so wholesome, as Allen became closer to the entire King family. So close, in fact, that an immediate member of Rodney King's family was one of Pooh's companions the night in February 1984 when Allen used verbal threats and a can of mace to rob a McDonald's restaurant in the San Fernando Valley.

While fleeing the scene of the robbery, Allen was shot in a leg and a foot by police officers and spent slightly more than a week in a jail hospital before going to trial. Pooh Allen, Rodney King's close relative, and another youth wound up doing not quite two and a half years in prison for that robbery adventure.

This was in addition to other jail terms Allen had served for robbery, receiving stolen property, and being drunk in public, not counting an arrest at age thirteen for assault with a deadly weapon and another arrest on the same charges a couple of years later for hitting a schoolteacher with a blackjack.

Allen is worth this minor diversion because he played a supporting role in the drama that occurred on March 3, 1991. Allen was one of two passengers in the car with Rodney King that night.[17]

Unlike King, Allen and the other passenger obeyed officers' commands to exit the automobile and lie down to be cuffed. Both Allen and the other passenger were released without being taken into custody, since they had committed no obvious offenses that night. Allen, though, objected to being turned loose in an area of known gang activity, although he testified in a sworn deposition that he had never associated with gang members and thus presumably had no reason to be worried.

Later, Allen would join King in suing the city and the officers. He told a psychiatrist hired by his attorney that the cops had kicked him "a number of times on the right side of the chest and the ribcage area and thigh," an accusation nobody except maybe the psychiatrist believed and certainly not sustained by portions of the

Holliday videotape that never made network television or by a second tape of the incident, which few people know about and will be discussed later.

Allen said that hearing Rodney King's "bones cracking" accompanied by screams—which were not audible on the enhanced audio portion of the Holliday videotape—had given him "bad dreams," made him "paranoid," and caused "severe [emotional] trauma," according to psychiatric records filed with the court in connection with the case.

Part of that "trauma," Allen told his psychiatrist, was due to being set free the night of March 3 in a neighborhood said to be controlled by the "Crips," an infamous street gang, since he had once been active in the rival "Bloods" gang—an admission at 180-degree odds with his sworn depositions. Not only that, he told the psychiatrist, but memories of the incident had caused him almost to double his consumption of alcohol, now more than fifteen quarts of beer a week. He freely acknowledged robbing the McDonald's, but said nothing about any resulting "trauma" from being shot comparable with what he experienced after March 3, 1991. It was a curious lapse. One would imagine that being shot twice by police would be far more traumatic than simply being handcuffed and released.

But multiple lawsuits were in the works with the Rodney King incident. And so, not surprisingly, the psychiatrist reported to Allen's attorney that Allen had developed "significant psychiatric difficulty following this traumatic, brutalizing, life-threatening event" of March 3, 1991. The psychiatrist found Allen to be "temporarily totally disabled" and recommended "supportive psychotherapy" at least once weekly for three to six months. Clearly, the table Rodney King had prepared was capable of producing enough crumbs to spread around for almost everybody to get a share.[18]

Rodney King's rap sheet doesn't reflect behavior as naughty as Pooh Allen's, but it's bad enough to stand out in a crowd of petty criminals. Among the offenses for which he had been arrested prior to March 3, 1991, were solicitation of prostitution—he offered the undercover Pasadena vice-squad female only $5 to perform oral sex, a frugal if not downright stingy proposition. In addition there was a charge of tampering with a vehicle, two counts of assault with a deadly weapon intending to inflict great bodily harm, and one accusation of spousal abuse.

No worthwhile purpose would be served here by detailing all of these charges except for one, which deals directly with character and Rodney King's accusations of police racism.

On July 27, 1987, King's wife at the time, Denatta King, called the Los Angeles County Sheriff's Department to complain that her husband had beaten her. The investigating deputy reported as follows:

> The victim said she was asleep in her bed when the suspect (husband) walked in her house and drug [*sic*] her out of bed. The suspect started striking the victim about her face with his fists. While striking the victim the suspect told her he wanted her car and she better give him the car keys.

At this point, someone else, apparently a Sheriff's Department supervisor, had added to the report: "The victim and suspect do not live together."

The investigating deputy's report continued: "The suspect then drug [*sic*] the victim outside of the house and continued to strike her about the face and chest areas.... While talking with the victim I noticed she had blood coming from her upper lip (1/4" laceration). She also had a scratch on the right side of her neck and a swollen right eye.... The suspect was transported to the station and booked."

Now, by itself this is unfortunately a relatively common report of alleged domestic violence. But its significance surfaced in depositions taken for Rodney King's civil suit against the city of Los Angeles. It demonstrated a strain of bigotry within Rodney King that was absent from the officers' conduct on March 3, 1991, even though the government probed endlessly (and unsuccessfully) to find one. Apparently, it was OK with the government if Rodney King was a bigot.

You see, when asked under oath about the spousal-abuse incident and whether he had "touched" his wife, King answered:

"They were... at one point there was a little pushing. And I pushed her. *And she was a high yellow, and you barely have to touch them for them to bruise sometimes*" (emphasis added).

The regional dialectic subtlety was apparently lost on the Los Angeles lawyers, although it's amazing that the government's civil rights lawyers didn't pick up on it. That's because "high yellow" is a racist term used in the South by some black and white people alike to describe African Americans of predominantly white bloodlines. Bigots especially like the phrase. If a white person calls a black person a "high yellow," it is an insulting, racist comment, suggesting that anything less than lily white is somehow inferior. It is just as bad if not worse for a black person to use the term. An African American who calls another a "high yellow" is the equivalent of a white person calling a black person a "nigger." And to say that a "high yellow" bruises easily is not much different, if any, from a white bigot saying that all blacks have rhythm or any other racially ascribed trait that ignores individual differences. *"And she was a high yellow, and you barely have to touch them for them to bruise sometimes."* It is nothing less than outright racism, pure and simple. And Rodney King said it.

Denatta King declined to pursue the battery charge against her husband, and he was released. Indeed, King was repeatedly able to dodge the bullets of prosecution and jail times. Two other domestic assault charges were never prosecuted by complainants, and the solicitation of prostitution charge, a misdemeanor, resulted in nothing more than a citation, the equivalent of a minor traffic ticket.

But King's luck ran out in late 1989, when he was arrested on a charge of second degree robbery. The offense was described in a probation officer's report:

> On Friday, Nov. 3, 1989, at approximately noon defendant (King) enters a small market in Monterey park. He picks up a package of [chewing] gum and hands the clerk, a 41-year-old male Korean, Tac Suck Baik, $1 in food coupons. The clerk then gives the defendant his change.
>
> At this time the defendant pulls a tire iron from his waistband and tells the clerk to open the cash register. The clerk does so and begins pulling money out.... The clerk asks the defendant not to take any checks from the cash register. The defendant, who is six-foot-three and weighs 220 pounds, attempts to strike the clerk, who is five-eight and weighs 175 pounds, with the tire iron.

> The clerk grabs the tire iron and the defendant loses his balance and falls behind the counter. A struggle ensues. The defendant then knocks over a large display case and then climbs back over to the other side of the counter. He picks up a piece of the display rack and tries to hit the clerk. The clerk then runs to the rear of the store and the defendant runs out the front door. The clerk gets the license number of the defendant's car and notifies the police. The police report indicates that the clerk sustained cuts and abrasions to his right arm, left wrist and left knee.

The original charge included assault with a deadly weapon, but that count was dropped "in furtherance of justice," an official leniency Rodney King has found highly advantageous since he became a race-victim poster child after his videotaped arrest. And so, on February 8, 1990, King was sentenced to two years' imprisonment.

King insisted he was blameless in the matter. The display case that was knocked over contained snack pies, and King said the incident was nothing more than a "pie-throwing" contest. But King was unable to explain away the checks made out to the retail store that were found in the glove box of the automobile he was driving when arrested.

Even so, the legal system was to blame for his conviction on the robbery charge, King complained in the November 1993 deposition. "If I had a proper, you know, legal system behind me, by the time that I had the... the first time getting in trouble[19] and they had me pleading to guilty.... I had to go and settle for a public defender. I didn't have the money to afford a real attorney... so I pled guilty to a robbery."

King served not quite half of the two-year sentence. He was released in December 1990. Three months later he tried to run from the cops, resisted arrest, got beaten, and was transformed into a folk hero by the George Holliday videotape.

In his new victim status—a symbol of police racial oppression—King became even more bulletproof than before. During the months following March 3, 1991, King was arrested again for drunken driving, charged again by his wife (a new one, Crystal King) with spousal abuse, and, in another revealing lapse of character, accused of trying to run over two vice-squad cops who caught him in the compromising company of a male transvestite prostitute. The probation officer's report on the incident read as follows:

On 5-28-91, at approximately 23:15 hours [11:15 P.M.], parolee King was observed by undercover officers E. Baeza and L. Chavez to pick up a female impersonator (Martinez, Hector) in an area that is known for prostitution. The officers continued to monitor parolee King's vehicle and they observed it pull to the rear of 4305 Gateway St.... and park underneath a parking stall. The officers continued to surveil the vehicle to determine if an unlawful act was about to occur.

As Officer Baeza watched the vehicle, he states that he observed parolee King and suspect Martinez recline their seats back. He also states that he observed Martinez place his head and shoulders in King's groin area. At this point, Officer Baeza prepared to approach the vehicle to ascertain if a lewd act was occurring. Officer Baeza placed his badge in his left hand, shouted "Police Officer" and approached the vehicle.

Parolee King noticed an individual approaching his vehicle and he reacted by starting his truck. He feared that he had been set up, and that he was going to be robbed and shot.... Next he placed it in reverse and quickly backed up. He then quickly placed the vehicle in drive and immediately sped off.

As parolee King drove off, the vehicle came close to one of the officers. They [the vice squad cops] stated that the vehicle came within 1–2 feet of Officer Chavez. Therefore they drew their weapons and pointed them toward the vehicle. However, no shots were fired.

A few moments later, King returned with a marked patrol unit, which he had asked to follow him. He had contacted the unit and told them that someone tried to rob and shoot him. He was taken into custody and released.

In addition to these incidents, as a parolee King had to be tested routinely for narcotics. He failed twice in the spring of 1991, with positive results for cocaine on May 29 and for heroin two weeks later. In testimony and depositions, King acknowledged a one-time use of cocaine but denied taking heroin; he claimed he had been ingesting percodan, a prescription painkiller necessary, he said, as a result of the injuries he claimed to have received during the March 3 incident. King said he also took the drugs to relieve "stress" imposed by reading the massive Christopher Commission report on race relations that the Los Angeles Police Department compiled after the 1992 riots. Perhaps so, but anyone who's ever scanned the report's thousands of pages will suspect that even heroin would be insufficient help in absorbing it for someone with the reading skills of a third grader.

King's attorney, Lerman, complained to the press that police officers were persecuting his client with all of these arrests. It's true that King was getting special attention, but it was far from negative. On the contrary, persuasive evidence suggests that he was receiving kid-glove treatment precisely because he was *the* Rodney King.

When his wife complained that he had abused her, the LAPD sent a high-ranking commander—in fact, a deputy chief—out to supervise a case that usually would have been handled by a patrol officer.[20] The drunken driving charges were dropped. And the state declined to revoke his parole for the demonstrable violation that occurred on March 3, 1991, despite King's own admissions of guilt.

A review of King's status was conducted by a probation officer on December 9, 1991, with the recommendation that he remain on supervised parole. The reviewing officer dryly noted: "Parolee King's re-entry into the community has been quite eventful."

But on December 27, 1991, after the Simi Valley trial and Los Angeles riots, the California Department of Corrections removed King from supervision despite another drunken driving charge on July 16 of that year and the two failed drug tests. The probation officer said in a written report that King "has become a much more responsible and mature individual.... [He] has completed a successful second year on parole and discharge consideration is warranted."

Indeed, the Teflon-like coating that has protected Rodney King from the law since March 3, 1991, seems to have grown even stronger. He was arrested on another drunken driving charge in June 1995, this time in Pennsylvania where he was visiting to attend the funeral of Crystal King's father.[21]

A few weeks later, in Alhambra, California, the more serious charge of assault with a deadly weapon/automobile was leveled against King after he and his wife got in a dispute while driving. He pulled over to the roadside. She got out of the car and reportedly was reaching back in for her purse when he sped away, knocking her to the ground and inflicting injuries that required hospital treatment. The Alhambra police didn't formally take Rodney King into custody until an officer arrived with a videocamera to get a film record of the arrest. Taking Rodney King into custody had become almost a cottage industry among police officers in Southern California, but you had to have a videocamera to do the job properly. The cops were learning, even if Rodney King wasn't.[22]

Matters of character. Stacey Koon and Rodney King. The contrast couldn't be more vivid. Koon is out of jail after serving all of the required time for an offense he arguably didn't commit. King has been in jail once already for a felony offense he did commit, but ever since has walked every time he was arrested. He faces another trial for an alleged assault on his wife in July 1995. If convicted on that charge, he could be headed for serious trouble. California has a "three strikes and you're out" law—which puts people in prison for life without possibility of parole for three felony convictions. Rodney King's almost halfway out of the batter's box.

Given Stacey Koon's background and character, it was inevitable that before March 3, 1991, he would once again encounter, as he had before, a violent offender who would resist being taken into custody. After all, arresting street thugs was his job as a police officer. And given his character and record of performance over almost fifteen years, it was predictable that he would strictly follow the rules in making the arrest.

Similarly, given Rodney King's background and character, it seems almost equally inevitable before March 3, 1991, that he would again get in trouble with the law and react the way he did—irrationally— and try to avoid an arrest that was going to happen regardless of his actions, explanations, alibis, and lies.

The sense of inevitability is what makes the story resemble a Greek tragedy, a drama destined to devastate the lives of both principal characters and thousands of other innocent people. The opening scene of the drama came shortly after midnight on March 3, 1991, on the right-hand shoulder of a curved portion of Foothill Boulevard near the entrance to Hansen Dam Recreational Park.

IV

REVISITING MARCH 3, 1991, AND ITS AFTERMATH

It's now [just] a matter of identifying witnesses.

Los Angeles Mayor Tom Bradley
March 5, 1991

The Arrest of Rodney King

America generally felt good about itself as the nation entered the first weekend in March 1991.

The Gulf War was over. The mood largely was euphoric over a sweeping military victory. Casualties in the war had been light, victory complete under the objectives laid out by the United Nations mandate. Haunting memories of Vietnam were being laid to rest.

On the civilian front, the Dow Jones industrial average closed on Friday, March 2, at 2909.9, the highest level since the prior autumn. President George Bush had an approval rating of 91 percent, the highest in recorded U.S. history and appeared unbeatable for reelection in 1992. In a political analysis of the race for the Democratic presidential nomination, the *Los Angeles Times* Washington bureau speculated that little-known Arkansas Governor Bill Clinton placed next to last in a list of candidates headed by Tennessee Senator Al Gore.

In Los Angeles, the weather was brisk, with temperatures on Saturday night, March 2, bottoming out in the mid-40s. A lingering drought had required water-rationing in Los Angeles recently, but a third consecutive day of rainfall—downtown LA got more than half an inch—provided hope that the shortage soon would be over.

In the northern part of the city, residents of apartments along Foothill Boulevard near Hansen Dam Recreational Park had enjoyed an exciting week. Although the film capital of the world, even *Angelenos* were captivated by movie stars, and some of the area residents had acquired videocameras to take pictures of Arnold Schwarzenegger, who had been in the neighborhood for the past several days to film scenes for a new movie that had generated a lot of advance publicity. It was called *The Terminator.*

Farther to the north, in a suburb beyond the Magic Mountain theme park, Sergeant Stacey Koon had spent Saturday morning sleeping, then doing routine "Mr. Mom" chores with his five children and spending time with his wife, Mary, who was off for the weekend from her job as a registered nurse.

After getting the kids to bed, Koon prepared to go to work at the Foothill Division of the Los Angeles Police Department, where he was a supervisor on the 11:00 P.M. to 7:00 A.M. shift. The prior shift's supervisor needed to leave before 11:00 P.M. and had asked Koon to relieve him earlier than usual. Once at the Foothill Station a few minutes before eleven o'clock, Koon began going through the red tape necessary to sustain a modern police bureaucracy. Koon, exercising his command prerogative, shelved the shift's nightly roll call and training session to complete the official paperwork. The training that night was on the appropriate and effective use of the PR 24 baton to subdue a resisting suspect. Koon had extensive training and experience in supervising uses of force involving the PR 24 baton, which is a metal pipe about two feet long with an L-shaped handle that permits an officer additional leverage and striking power. One of the officers on Koon's shift, Patrolman Laurence Powell, had difficulty swinging the pipe effectively at the rubber-encased post that represented a suspect; Powell was taken aside for additional instruction.

At this time, shortly after 11:00 P.M., about forty miles to the southeast in the Altadena neighborhood of Pasadena, Rodney King was in the driver's seat of his wife's car, a 1988 Hyundai Excel. The car was parked in the darkened driveway of an acquaintance, Freddy Helms. Helms was in the front passenger's seat, and King's boyhood friend, Pooh Allen, was seated in the back. The amplifier-boosted radio was thundering out rap, and King, Allen, and Helms were shucking and jiving along with the staccato lyrics. They were all drinking from forty-ounce bottles of Old English 800 malt liquor, a brew more potent than beer.

The drinking had begun almost six hours earlier, around 5:30 P.M., when Allen arrived at King's house to watch a ball game on television. They started with cans of beer, but ran out about 7:00 P.M. King and Allen went to a liquor store, where they graduated to the larger containers of malt liquor, and then picked up Freddy Helms.

Around 11:30 P.M., King said he wanted to visit Hansen Dam Recreational Park where his father had once taken him fishing. That's not the same story Pooh Allen told; according to Allen they were going to look for female companionship—"look for women," as he testified. Yet a third version was that they were going to buy more beer.

Consistency, though, has been an elusive element throughout Rodney King's version of the saga. What is known is that shortly before midnight on Saturday, March 2, Rodney King was drunk, with a blood-alcohol level estimated by later measurements to be 0.19 percent, or more than twice the legal limit for driving in California.

King, Allen, and Helms set off on their journey, headed northwest on the 210 Freeway, also known as the Foothill Freeway, toward the Hansen Dam Recreational Park. By the time they neared the Sunland Boulevard exit, their speed had reached more than one hundred miles per hour, according to California Highway Patrol (CHP) reports. The car's boom box was still blasting, which might account for Rodney King's inability to hear police sirens, at least at first, although it doesn't explain how he was able to ignore his rearview mirror reflecting the flashing red lights of the CHP cruiser in pursuit.

Fewer than five miles away, Sergeant Koon had completed his paperwork and was leaving the station house for field patrol. As he got in his black-and-white, as Los Angeles cops refer to their cruisers, he heard the police radio broadcast a message that the California Highway Patrol, which had been joined by a unit from the Los Angeles Unified School District (LAUSD) police force, was in a high-speed chase of a vehicle. Koon turned his black-and-white in the direction the chase seemed to be leading—the directions provided by the pursuit vehicle were not altogether accurate and somewhat confusing—and raced toward the scene of the action.

A collision of characters and values was about to occur. It was a clash that would produce shock waves across the world, one that would make America feel not so good about itself for months to come. The lives of tens of thousands of people would forever be altered, and no one would be more affected than Stacey Koon and Rodney King. No one, except perhaps the people killed, crippled, and otherwise devastated in the Los Angeles riots. And it all happened because Rodney King got drunk, got caught driving, and didn't want to go back to jail for violating his parole.

The important basic facts of what happened when Koon and King's destinies clashed shortly after midnight on Sunday, March 3, 1991, are not in dispute.[1]

King brought his car to a stop at the entrance to Hansen Dam Recreational Park. He said he stopped voluntarily, although he had ignored plenty of earlier opportunities to pull over during the course of the police pursuit, which took place at speeds of up to and more than one hundred miles per hour, according to the CHP's account of the incident. In fact, he had stopped briefly once, then started up again and driven a few hundred more yards before finally rolling to a halt.

Perhaps King did stop voluntarily. But a better case can be made that King stopped only because the entrance to the park had been closed with a thick chain and he was unable to gain entry to the recreational park. The argument that he didn't stop of his own free will is buttressed by King himself, who said he was trying to avoid being returned to prison for parole violations; he could lose the cops more easily in the wooded park where his vehicle was clearly headed.

But the park entrance was sealed, and by the time his vehicle had rolled to a stop, so had the cops' pursuit cruisers, and his Hyundai was blocked from going either forward or backward. Six police officers (by this time LAPD unit A-23 occupied by Powell and Wind had joined the original CHP and LAUSD patrol cars) were standing behind the doors of their cars, guns drawn and pointed at the Hyundai. Escape into the park would have been impossible.

King ignored orders to exit the vehicle. He later testified that he had gotten entangled in the seatbelt and couldn't get out as commanded. Allen and Helms both obeyed orders to get out of the car and lie facedown on the ground; they were immediately handcuffed without resistance or injury, although Allen later claimed severe "trauma."

When King did get out of the car he danced around, pointing at the police helicopter hovering closely overhead, its flaring light illuminating the scene below. At this point Koon arrived, pulling his cruiser to the front and slightly left of King's vehicle to prevent any escape back onto the roadway. It was a position that gave Koon a clear view of King, one that allowed him to develop a tactic in case King resisted arrest—normal police procedure for a nighttime chase.

Then King grabbed his buttocks and shook them in a mocking, perhaps even suggestive sexual, manner at an approaching officer, CHP Patrolwoman Melanie Singer, who was advancing with her gun drawn. In later testimony and interviews, King denied the conduct. But it was confirmed by so many other people present that Judge Davies accepted the officers' version as truthful. (The corollary of which, of course, is that King was lying. But in view of the later interviews with FBI agents and other investigators and courtroom testimony as well, the untruths and half-truths he would tell, the lie was so insignificant as to be almost meaningless in the larger scheme of matters.)

The next sequence of events occurred with almost fast-forward timing, occupying the final few seconds before George Holliday turned his videocamera on the scene from his balcony at the Lakeview Terrace Apartments more than one hundred yards away.

King continued to refuse to obey police commands to get on the ground, to put his face down, to put his hands in the small of his back. It was the appropriate set of commands to give to a suspected felony evader, a category into which King neatly fit because of his obvious attempts to evade the police pursuit.[2] Melanie Singer continued to approach King with her gun drawn. It was a dangerous situation in Koon's view. Los Angeles Police Department rules forbade advancing on a suspect with a drawn pistol unless it was a life-threatening situation; the accessibility of a pistol is how police officers and suspects alike can get hurt or killed.

So Koon, by now in command and joined by another LAPD unit occupied by Briseno and probationary officer Rolando Solano, ordered Singer and all of the other officers present to holster their weapons. He told Singer to back away from the suspect.

As Melanie Singer retreated, King began making a clicking sound with his tongue and palate. It was a "tsk, tsk, tsk" sound, not one of regret but almost like a series of hisses.

To an inexperienced civilian, the gesture is meaningless. But to a cop it is significant in evaluating a suspect's attitude, because in prison it is associated with contempt, even defiance, by convicts for their jailers. A prisoner cannot be openly abusive to a guard. The "tsk, tsk, tsk" sound is one way a prisoner can say to a guard, "Fuck you."

Rodney King had been out of prison only three months, and in jailhouse jargon he was telling the cops what he thought of them. It was defiance. Koon and the other officers did not know that King was a recent ex-con, but they suspected him to be one for several reasons.[3] And the "tsk, tsk, tsk" defiance provided another clue. By itself, the defiance wasn't too bad. But together with other behavioral patterns King displayed that night, it suggested to Koon that he intended to resist arrest physically.

Los Angeles Police Department rules require a field commander to use his or her own officers to take a suspect into custody if the LAPD is in charge of an arrest attended by officers from other jurisdictions (in this case the CHP, which initiated the pursuit, and the LAUSD officers who joined it). The reason is that a commanding officer must be able to predict how a team of cops will react in a specific situation. LAPD training and procedures are uniform, and in some ways different from other law-enforcement agencies, as demonstrated by Melanie Singer's approaching King with a drawn pistol.

So Koon had to rely only on the LAPD officers at the scene—and at this time, just four had arrived—to take King into custody. Unless an emergency situation developed, he would be unable to employ Melanie Singer and her partner/training officer, CHP Patrolman Tim Singer (also Melanie's husband), or the LAUSD officers. Koon directed his orders to Powell, Wind, Briseno, and Solano.

To King, he continued issuing verbal commands, the second level of a graduated use-of-force response to a suspect's actions. (The first is physical presence, and it's difficult to imagine a more conspicuous visible presence than eight officers from four squad cars, all with flashing red lights, and a police helicopter overhead illuminating the scene.) "Get down," Koon ordered King. "Put your face on the pavement. Put your hands behind your back." It was all standard LAPD procedure in arresting a felony suspect.

For a moment, it appeared as though King was going to comply with Koon's orders. King got down on his hands and knees. But it wasn't the position of a suspect obeying orders to get into a face-down prone position. It was more like a "runner on the starting blocks" position, Koon said, suggesting to a veteran police officer that attack or flight was imminent.

Koon was thus faced with an unsearched felony suspect who appeared about to assault the officers or flee, neither option obviously acceptable. In fact, the officers would be breaking the law themselves if they voluntarily allowed a suspect to avoid detention.

If King attacked, either the suspect or an officer was liable to get hurt, perhaps killed.

If a gun somehow got taken away from an officer, a cop, King, or an innocent civilian member of the crowd now gathering nearby could get hurt, maybe killed.

If King successfully escaped, he might hurt himself or someone else later on. Something had to be done—and quickly.

The situation was getting out of hand—and Rodney King so far was controlling every second of it with his actions.

Koon then issued an order that later became a central issue in the federal criminal trial. Using verbal commands and body language, he directed the four LAPD officers present—Powell, Wind, Briseno, and Solano—to approach King and force him physically to the ground, wrench his arms behind his back, and finally restrain him with handcuffs.

The order was not an official "swarm," as government prosecutors later argued. Indeed, it couldn't have been a "swarm," because the Los Angeles Police Department had never had such a policy. Granted, some experienced street cops used an unofficial "team take-down" technique when necessary. This utilitarian technique involves the use of the chokehold to subdue a combative suspect. The chokehold is an embrace of a suspect's neck and upper body area. The upper body is restrained with one arm, and the person applying the pressure uses the other arm's bone structure in the wrist area to cut off the flow of oxygen-rich blood through the carotid artery to the brain. Unconsciousness quickly results, usually within two to four seconds. But even this technique had been discouraged almost ten years earlier when the Los Angeles Police Commission, backed by the City Council, outlawed use of chokeholds because of complaints by minority leaders that the chokeholds were being used too frequently and lethally on minority suspects.

The political and legal ramifications of abandoning the chokehold is explored in more detail later in this book. Suffice it to say here, in this brief account of the March 3, 1991, incident, that before escalating to another level of force Koon wanted to exhaust all available remedies. But a "swarm," or officially approved team take-down, wasn't one of them. That is because it had never existed and, in fact, didn't come into existence until after the officers had been convicted. Blaming the cops for not using an officially sanctioned swarm on Rodney King would be like blaming FDR for not dropping an atomic bomb on the Japanese on December 8, 1941, to retaliate for Pearl Harbor—it couldn't be done, because it didn't exist.

But Koon could try a modified team take-down, which is a technique that is used sometimes, even though it was not officially part of the LAPD training manual at that time. So that is what Koon ordered. Using verbal commands and body language, Koon directed Powell, Wind, Briseno, and Solano to approach King and surround him. Powell grabbed King's left arm; Briseno, King's right arm. Wind reached for King's right leg; Solano, the left. Powell and Wind tried to force King's arms behind his back, but King resisted—his arms were "like steel poles," Koon said. Then, suddenly, King straightened out his arms and Powell and Briseno slammed the suspect's face into the pavement. It was violent and brutal, but it was legal.

Then something happened that worried Koon. King thrust out one arm, and Powell was thrown off. Then the other arm moved jerkily, and Briseno was shoved away. King shook his legs and Wind and Solano went tumbling. From the beginning, Koon had suspected that King was high on something. The initial suspicion was PCP, "angel dust," a powerful human stimulant originally developed as a tranquilizer for animals. It is not known whether he had taken PCP that night, and King denies that he did.[4] However, he was more than twice legally drunk and had used marijuana at some time in the recent past, although Koon and the officers could not have known that at the time.

But they didn't have to possess that knowledge, just as they didn't have to know whether King was armed since they hadn't had a chance to search his waistband, pockets, socks, and other places where weapons can be concealed. The reason was that King *was acting* as if he were on PCP by displaying the remarkable, almost inhuman, strength the drug provides, and he *was acting* like a potentially dangerous felony suspect. So the officers had to respond as if he were both. To do otherwise would have been too perilous.

LAPD rules forbid tying up physically with a suspect if that procedure has already been tried and failed, so Koon ordered the four officers away from King and graduated to the next level of force: the TASER electric stunning device.[5] The TASER is a small device that looks like a flashlight and is about the size of a home telephone handset. It contains two electrically charged cartridges, each of which is capable of transmitting fifty thousand volts of low-amperage, nonlethal electricity into a subject. When pointed at a suspect and activated, the TASER shoots two wire-connected darts into the subject. The darts don't have to penetrate garments or even touch skin; contact with clothing is sufficient. At the Los Angeles police academy, the TASER is demonstrated by having nine recruits hold hands, one flanking the other along a single line. The TASER is then discharged into the clothing of the middle recruit, number five, and activated. Invariably, the primary receiver and most if not all of the other eight recruits are flattened to the ground, muscular functions immobilized a minute or so and for all practical purposes out of action.

From about five feet away, Koon aimed the TASER at King, pushed the button, and two darts flew out, connecting in King's shirt in the upper left-front shoulder area. The fifty thousand volts slammed into King's body and he fell to the ground. But only for a brief second. He almost immediately recovered before the officers could approach and began getting back on his feet, dangerously contradicting the training manual on the TASER. Koon pushed the button for the second cartridge, and two more darts were ejected, this time connecting in the back of King's shirt in the left shoulder-blade area. Again fifty thousand volts surged through the wires. And again King went down. And again King arose immediately before the officers could even get their handcuffs ready, much less approach the suspect.

It was at this point that George Holliday's videocamera began recording the incident across the street. (It was a new camera, and Holliday had yet to give it a tough assignment. Earlier in the evening, he'd practiced with such subjects as a cat licking its paws and other gentle domestic scenes.) If he'd turned the lens on the drama occurring across the street only a few moments before, perhaps the news media would have had a different story to tell, since it would have clearly revealed Rodney King's aggressive behavior and the officers' graduated responses.

At almost the moment the videotape began, King was seen rising from the ground and lunging at Powell, who had taken his PR 24 baton out of its belt loop and was holding it at the ready. It is unclear whether King was trying to escape or to attack Powell. King contended in trial testimony that he was trying to flee, a version accepted by Judge Davies since the videotape revealed only the action, not the intent. King can be granted the intent, since it is about the only consistency in his testimony—he was trying to escape the officers from the moment the pursuit began.

As King lunged toward him, Powell swung the baton, arguably striking King in the right side of the face. It was not an illegal blow. LAPD guidelines forbid head shots with a baton unless deadly force is necessary, but only if such blows are intentional. Accidental blows to the head and other extremely vulnerable body parts are permissible if they are not deliberate.

That's how Judge Davies saw the first baton blow. In his sentencing memorandum, Judge Davies wrote: "In view of Mr. King's sudden approach and Officer Powell's legitimate interest in stopping the hard-charging Mr. King, Officer Powell *may* have inadvertently struck his head. *Telling evidence that the head blow was unintentional is provided by the fact that Officer Powell never clearly applied force to Mr. King's head again, although he had ample opportunity to do so*" (emphasis added).

At this point Koon directed the officers to beat the suspect into submission—the next prescribed step in the graduated levels of force he was applying. Powell and Wind began striking King, delivering a "torrent" of blows to King's chest, thighs, and arms, to use Koon's description that night in his written report of the incident.

Even the baton blows were delivered in accordance with the official policy of escalating and deescalating physical force. The videotape makes it appear as though Powell and Wind were taking turns striking King. But that is a false impression. They would deliver a series of power strokes, say three or four, then step back to see if King would obey their repeated commands to prone out on his face with his hands behind his back. When King made a move that appeared to be another attempt to rise, they would then step in and deliver another series of blows, say five or six this time, upping the ante the suspect would have to pay for continued resistance, flight, or attack. It was a classic use of the baton under LAPD policies, procedures, and training.

Classic, except for one thing: Not all of the power strokes made contact with King—hardly flattering to the effectiveness of LAPD training with the PR 24 baton. Wind, for example, swung at King fifteen times and connected only eleven times. Powell, despite his extra training when the shift began, missed almost as many times as he hit during the eighty-two–second duration of the Holliday videotape that most television viewers saw.

Which might be one explanation why Rodney King kept trying to rise to his feet—he wasn't yet in enough pain to comply with police commands. Indeed, according to Judge Davies, King himself was responsible for the officers' responses for all but the last nineteen seconds of the incident.

Finally, with King still unfazed and continuing to resist obedience, Koon ordered Powell and Wind to strike King in his joints—elbows, knees, ankles, wrists. The idea was to inflict enough pain to force him to comply with commands to be taken into custody. Finally, King submitted. He sat back on his ankles, held his hands in the air, and said, "Please stop." It was an action he could have taken at any time during the prior eighty-two seconds.

King's compliance was not the end Koon had hoped for. King's face wasn't in the ground; he could still see the officers and form a plan of attack or flight. His hands were still free to strike an officer, his feet still unfettered and capable of kicking. But, as Koon later wrote, "at this point I was willing to take anything I could get from Rodney King."[6]

King was grabbed by at least seven officers, some of whom had just arrived at the scene. His hands were forced behind his back, and he was put in handcuffs, a double set of them—routine with PCP suspects, who have been known to break out of a single pair of alloy steel cuffs. His ankles were then tied to the handcuffs in what is known in police parlance as a "hog-tie" and carried—not dragged, as the videotape clearly reveals—to the roadside to await arrival of an ambulance to transport him to Pacifica Hospital for diagnosis and treatment of any injuries.

Koon designated Wind and Officer Susan Clemmer, a new cop only five days off her probationary period, to ride with King in the ambulance on its way to Pacifica Hospital. Clemmer's length of time on the LAPD, and what she said about Rodney King's behavior during the ambulance ride—she testified that King kept repeating "Fuck you," and spitting saliva mixed with traces of blood on her uniform trousers—figured later in showing how government prosecutors sought to intimidate witnesses.

But let's return to Pacifica Hospital. There, King was diagnosed by the attending physician as having overdosed on PCP, a diagnosis that could not be sustained (see endnote four to this chapter) and suffering from "superficial" facial lacerations. He left Pacifica under his own power, but under guard, headed for the Los Angeles County–University of Southern California Medical Center (LACUSCMC), where jailed suspects requiring medical observation or attention are housed in a ward on the thirteenth floor.[7] It transpired later that his injuries were more severe than the original diagnosis, but the officers only knew of the original analysis, which made a mockery of later accusations that they conspired to cover up the seriousness of King's injuries. The new medical knowledge wasn't available for another twenty-four hours or more. But these facts didn't inhibit either the state or federal prosecutors from trying to prove— unsuccessfully, of course—that a coverup existed.

For Koon and his officers, the incident was over, or so it would appear. The arrest was not routine—the level of force applied took it out of the routine category. But it certainly wasn't very uncommon for the LAPD or any other major metropolitan police force. So reports were made and filed. Koon, Powell, Wind, Briseno, Solano, Clemmer, and all of the other officers present at the arrest completed their shifts and went home, and Rodney King spent a painful first night in the hospital.

One of the cops, though, was having doubts. Or at least he later said he was having doubts. That was Theodore Briseno. Briseno became a key witness against the other cops in the state trial at Simi Valley, and his testimony there would be manipulated by U.S. attorneys in the subsequent federal prosecution.

At Simi Valley, Briseno testified that he believed the force used to subdue Rodney King was excessive. The Holliday videotape showed Briseno "stomping" on King at one point, but Briseno insisted that he was simply trying to get King to stay down and be handcuffed. Granted, Briseno is seen at one point holding up a baton to warn Powell away. Briseno said he did so because he wanted to stop the beating. Powell and Koon, though, interpreted the gesture differently; they said Briseno was warning Powell off because the TASER was still transmitting electrical pulsations into King's body, and if Powell touched King he'd get zapped by the voltage just like an academy cadet in training. And, in fact, Wind's memory is that he recalled Briseno warning them to get back or they'd get shocked by the TASER.

In any event, Briseno said he was so concerned about what he considered excessive force that he returned to the Foothill Station immediately after the incident to report the matter to senior watch officers for official action. Once at the station house, Briseno said, he saw a computer display terminal reporting a message from Koon to the duty lieutenant, Patrick Conmay, notifying the watch commander that Koon had just been involved in a use-of-force arrest. The message said: "U just had a big-time use of force. TASED and beat the suspect of CHP pursuit. Big time."[8] Since the message had already been delivered, Briseno testified, he turned around, left the station house, and resumed patrol for the rest of the shift.

A subtle but highly important matter of motivation is involved here. If Briseno believed the force employed on King was excessive and illegal, then it was altogether appropriate that he return to the Foothill Station to report it. But it logically follows from this that if he didn't return to the station house as he testified, then presumably he didn't regard the force as improper. Hence the truthfulness of his entire range of testimony about excessive force hinged on whether he returned to the Foothill Station to blow the whistle on Koon, Powell, and Wind.

Here's the dilemma for Briseno: The Foothill Station computer transmission operator testified at the Simi Valley trial that she immediately passed Koon's message on to the watch commander and then erased it. The message could not have remained on-screen for more than a couple of minutes, at most, before it was purged from the system.

In order for Briseno to return to the Foothill Station and see Koon's message while it was still on-screen in the watch commander's office, Briseno would have had to travel the two miles to the station at an average speed of eighty to ninety miles per hour on city streets following a route interrupted by four major intersections, not counting time to park his black-and-white, race into the station house, and enter the watch commander's office. The situation is not just implausible; it's impossible.

But that's not all of the evidence supporting the allegation that Briseno lied at Simi Valley.

A lot of people aren't aware of it, but George Holliday's videocamera wasn't the only one operating that night. The security guard at the Lakeview Terrace Apartments used one, too, and turned it on after Rodney King had been restrained. That videotape clearly shows Briseno's black-and-white still parked at the time Koon sent the message. And as soon as Koon transmitted the "U just had" communication, he returned directly to the station house to get a new

TASER, since the batteries in the one he carried had been depleted on Rodney King. Reason is defied by the proposition that Briseno left *after* Koon, but somehow got to the station *before* the sergeant arrived. Because, you see, Koon went straight to the station to check in with Lieutenant Conmay, who is one of several officers who saw Koon when he arrived. But not one of those present recalls seeing Briseno at the station house when Koon was there following the incident.

In short, Briseno lied at Simi Valley. And the federal government knew it.

But that Briseno scorned the truth wasn't important to federal prosecutors. Indeed, it provided them with leverage. Federal prosecutors believed they had Briseno nailed, whatever he said in the federal criminal trial. If he testified that he'd returned to the station house, they could make a solid, almost unbeatable case for perjury. If he said he hadn't gone to the station house, he'd be vulnerable as a defendant for using excessive force—and open to state perjury charges for his Simi Valley testimony.

Either way, the government appeared to have Briseno. That, one suspects, is the main reason why he took his chances and refused to testify at the federal criminal trial. But even a refusal to testify didn't bother government prosecutors. In fact, the prosecution team would find a way to capitalize on both the inconsistencies in Briseno's testimony at Simi Valley and his refusal to take the witness stand.

And so the background was set. The story of the government's willful, deliberate abuse of its powers at the altar of racial politics, an abuse abetted if not actively aided by the media, was about to begin.

Racial Politics

The media were slow to pick up on the Rodney King story. At first, that is.

The Holliday videotape was initially aired on the 10:00 P.M. news on KTLA-TV on Monday, March 4. By the next day it had been picked up by CNN. On Wednesday, the 6th, the *Los Angeles Times* reported that police were investigating the incident for possible excessive use of force. By Thursday, the 7th, the *Los Angeles Times* pulled all the plugs in its effort to play catch-up with television on a story that was essentially visual in nature—and incomplete, as well. Consider these small examples of how the story was portrayed by the *Times* almost from the beginning.

A March 8 piece by Metro columnist Al Martinez said that "Like Ku Klux Klanners on a feeding frenzy... twelve policemen took turns kicking and whacking him [King] with nightsticks." How Martinez came up with the figure twelve is unknown. And this, mind you, was written before the cops had a chance to tell their side of the story to their own department, much less the media.

Another story the same day reported as incontestable fact that "the officer who fired the [TASER] gun began hitting King with a nightstick." That officer was Sergeant Koon, and no one ever accused him of—nor did the videotape in any way show him—using any force other than the TASER on King.

A caricature by *Los Angeles Times* cartoonist Paul Conrad showed a defenseless man lying face down as five vicious police dogs tore at his clothing and flesh, blood pooling on the ground around his wounds. The image is wholly at odds with the reality of an aggressive, violent Rodney King resisting arrest.

And although it was already on everybody's minds, the matter of race was first raised in the media (except for minority leaders, who had already prejudged the incident as totally racial) by the *Los Angeles Times* editorial page, which put the episode in clear perspective just in case somebody had missed the point: "Because the victim was black, the incident inevitably raises questions about police and race relations in Los Angeles," the *Times* said before the week was out.

Aside from what is either casual disregard for truth or deliberate distortion of facts, the alarming result of such reporting and editorializing is the inflammatory effect it can have on public opinion. Consider some of the isolated words—"Ku Klux Klanners," "feeding frenzy," "kicking and whacking him with nightsticks." These phrases and the pictures they evoke could not have been intended to illuminate thought or understanding about an incident that was not as one-sided as everybody assumed and as the Holliday videotape had been edited to support. The media's performance, through dull ignorance or artful design, could not help but enrage people who had no evidence other than an incomplete videotape.

And make no mistake about it: If viewed carefully, and in the context of an understanding of Los Angeles Police Department policies, procedures, and training, the videotape clearly refutes prevailing media opinion. That was one reason for the innocent verdict in Simi Valley: The jury was able to view the Holliday videotape frame-by-frame in the overall context of Los Angeles Police Department rules. Contextual reference is where the media first fell down on the job, with ultimately devastating consequences.

One big reason for this lapse was that the command structure of the LAPD; the Los Angeles Police Commission, which establishes police policies; and the Los Angeles City Council, which endorses or rejects Police Commission recommendations, were all embarrassed by the Holliday videotape. Quite simply, the videotape revealed a fundamental weakness, a glaring gap, in policies the Police Commission wrote, the City Council approved, and the LAPD command structure implemented.

The Rodney King episode wasn't triggered by rogue cops out on a mission to beat a black man. The problem—quite free of racial designs—was embedded far more deeply within the police department and the Los Angeles political establishment. The politicians and LAPD commanders, if they were going to save themselves from criticism, needed sacrificial cops as much as or maybe even more than the media.

The tone was set by Mayor Tom Bradley, representing the political establishment, and Deputy Chief Robert Vernon, respresenting the LAPD. On March 5, Bradley went so far as to suggest that a trial wasn't even necessary. "It's now [just] a matter of identifying and finding witnesses," he said. Vernon, echoing that line at a March 8 news conference, expressed "outrage" at the incident, which he called a "horrible thing," and said he was "appalled and embarrassed" by it and "angry" with the officers involved. Everyone seemed to assume automatically that the incident was racial in nature, an assumption that persists although demonstrably false, as even the federal government admitted.

This last point illustrates a knotty little problem for those who wanted to play up the race angle: Everyone just assumed that the incident was rooted in race, but they assumed wrong.

And assumption is not proof. Never mind, though. Rodney King would be able to provide that evidence. Rodney King or his attorneys made certain that not just the race card but the entire deck would be shuffled and dealt early and often. It was intended to provide the trump suit in a civil action that might reap millions of dollars in damages for Rodney King—and millions for his lawyers, too.

King said at his first news conference in the hospital on Tuesday, March 5, that the incident was one of cops doing their job, that no racism was involved. He admitted drinking some, but not being drunk. He acknowledged that he ran because he didn't want to be arrested. According to Lerman, King didn't raise the race issue because "Mr. King and I decided not to exploit [it]... he declined to be part of the civil rights image."

Later the next day, when interviewed by the FBI, King told essentially the same story, although he was starting to embellish it somewhat.

In an interview with FBI Special Agent Jerry Delap on March 6, 1991, King outlined the background of beer-drinking with Freddy Helms and Pooh Allen, then described what happened after being stopped by the police.[9] Now let the internal report on the interview speak for itself:

> King stated that his maximum speed on the freeway was between 65 and 80 miles an hour, certainly no more than 80, and his speed along Osborne [a city street], after leaving the freeway, was probably between 45 and 50. He stated that he did not attempt to evade police officers through high speed and reckless driving and, in fact, immediately pulled over as soon as he was aware he was being stopped by the police.
>
> After stopping, a male police officer called to him to place his hands where they could be seen, on top of the steering wheel. He was then commanded to place his hands higher, in front of the windshield. He was commanded to open the door with his left hand, get out of the car and lay down on the ground. *He complied with all of these demands* [emphasis added].
>
> After laying on the ground, a female police officer ordered him to spread his arms and legs and he complied. He also was ordered, several times, to put his face on the ground.

As he lay on the ground, he was handcuffed with his hands behind his back and his feet were tied to his handcuffs. After he had been thus secured, he was approached by a white male officer who bent down and pushed something into his right shoulder. KING then received an electrical shock from this instrument which felt as though he was being touched by a live spark-plug wire but the shocking was sustained rather than instantaneous. After being shocked for four or five seconds, the instrument was removed from his shoulder and KING was struck on the head by some object. The instrument was then applied to KING's left shoulder and he was shocked again for a few seconds.

The officers then began beating KING and he received blows over most of his body. During the beating, he recalls going into a dazed condition where he did not feel pain from the blows [emphasis added].

King then told the FBI investigator that he was not under the influence of any drug or alcohol at any time during the incident and said he'd consumed only a partial bottle of beer earlier in the evening. He also denied resisting the officers "in any way, maintaining that he followed their commands and instructions at all times."

The FBI investigator concluded that King "seemed to have difficulty answering questions… and… remembering events and the sequence of events." According to the FBI agent, King's attorney explained that this was a result of "suffering from neurological damage."

That's a good answer, and one that for some reason apparently played well with the FBI. But it's false. The simple, provable fact is that King was already lying about the incident. The videotape clearly showed he was lying. The videotape showed that he was never handcuffed or hog-tied until the very end of the incident. He was not shot with the TASER until after he had thrown off four officers who were trying to put him in handcuffs, this last fact later proven in sworn testimony although not picked up on the videotape. In any event, the FBI agent should have known King was lying if the agent had bothered to give the Holliday videotape an even cursory examination before interviewing King. If the agent had seen the tape, then he bought into King's lies for some inexplicable reason.

Moreover, Rodney King himself later testified that he had consumed considerably more than a "partial" bottle of beer, and medical tests conducted at Pacifica Hospital, the results of which were available to the FBI, showed that at the time the incident occurred King's blood-alcohol level was more than twice the legal limit for a driving-while-drunk conviction in California.

In short King lied to the FBI. He told lie after lie after lie. And the FBI bought into the lies, or at least didn't contest them, although plenty of evidence proving King's untruthful statements was readily available. Instead, the FBI treated the demonstrably false statements as substantiated complaints.

Already it was becoming clear that truth was unimportant in this case. The videotape showed white cops beating a black man. Therefore, civil rights violations must have occurred.

The media and minority leaders, along with politicians of all stripes—conservative as well as liberal, Republican as well as Democratic—were shouting that this was a civil rights case, implying or saying outright that it was racially inspired. White cops beat a black man, hence race was the cause. Perception was important, not truth. And so began the federal government's abuse of power, less than three days after Rodney King violated numerous laws to avoid going back to prison.

King's actions suggest that it didn't take him long to realize that the racial angle was essential to nailing the cops on a criminal charge, which would, of course, be extremely helpful to any civil suit for monetary damages he might file.

Consequently, King began manufacturing more details to add to his story when interviewed in June 1991 by investigators Frank Oliver and Ken Godinas from the Los Angeles District Attorney's office, which was gathering "evidence" to support a criminal trial of the officers in state court.

King told Oliver and Godinas that when stopped he complied fully with officers' commands to get on the ground. But based on what King said he heard the officers saying, it became clear that "they wanted to blow my fucking brains out, man."

The incident was frightening, King told the investigators, because so many cops were involved. How many? Godinas asked.

"Shit, I know I was getting my ass kicked by about five," King responded. "I watched the rest of them come, and I watched the rest of them sit around this whole, it looked like a big block to me. It was a fucking block party was what it looked like to me. I could see them all around. And I'm wondering like, damn, why don't somebody stop them, man, why don't somebody stop them? Why don't one of these guys stop them and I could see them all around kinda' like smiling, looking at me like I was, like I was real shit, man, and then somebody walked over to me and laughed, after I was on the ground and down on the ground somebody walked over to me.

"Okay, well I layed [*sic*] down, face down...." King went on to the investigators. "I could see them walking over to me... boom, kicked me in my face, and then I heard, I heard, uh, we're going to kill you nigger, and..."

Now King had the investigators' attention. "You heard somebody say that?" Godinas asked.

"Yeah...." King responded. "I'm going to kill you nigger, run, like that. That's when I said, ah, shit, something ain't right.... [Because] I had no intention of running when, until he, uh, until I heard that, we're going to kill you, to a blow to the head, and then we're going to kill you nigger, run."

The investigators kept coming back to what King said he heard that night. In fact, you might almost call it leading the witness to develop some evidence of racial motivation on the officers' part. Godinas interrupted King's description of going "numb" from the TASER to ask, "Remember, GLENN, what was being said? Can you remember?"

King, now apparently getting the message, happily complied. "Yeah. Um, how you feel now, nigger, what's up nigger, how you feel now, killer, what's up killer, how you feel now? You know what I mean, just... little punk voices."

So clearly race was an issue. Rodney King had finally dotted the *i* and crossed the *t* for investigators. In fact, now race was probably *the* issue, just as it had been all along to critics of the officers' actions that night. And it wasn't just Rodney King saying it (or not saying it, depending upon the audience).

You see, the racial factor was essential to validate minority condemnations of whites as a whole, of police activity in Los Angeles generally, and of the Rodney King incident in particular. Without race, there was no issue at all. But there was a problem in acquiring the necessary proof beyond Rodney King's dubious statements. The problem was this: No one, at any time, under any circumstances, with any evidence, could state that Rodney King was stopped and beaten because he was a black man. Never was any proof of racial motivation offered, except in Rodney King's ambivalent, contradictory, and untruthful statements to investigators and his testimony on the witness stand.

In fact, all available facts suggested otherwise. For example: In preparation for the Simi Valley trial, the defense had the audio portion of the Holliday videotape enhanced electronically. This meant that technicians were able to use electronic wizardry to block out all sound-wave bands that carried extraneous background noise—the helicopter's whapping rotor blades, noises from the gathering crowd, police sirens, and so on—and allow the audio portion of the Holliday videotape to relay only those portions that recorded human voices. Most of those voices were police officers issuing commands. And those commands did not say "nigger," or "killer," or anything even resembling the racial trigger words that Rodney King claimed to investigators the police had used that night. What the cops said was this, as taken from the enhanced audio portion of the tape:

> *Put your hands behind your back.*
> *Hands behind your back.*
> *Just lay down.*
> *Behind your back.*
> *Lay on the ground.*
> *You've gotta put your hands out now.*
> *Put your hands out.*
> *Get your arms out.*
> *Put your arms out.*
> *He's comin' up.*
> *You're gonna get shot, you're gonna get shot.*
> *Keep your arms spread out.*
> *Stop…*
> *Roll over…*
> *Get down.*
> *Come in from the back.*
> *Cuff him.*

Put your hands behind your back.

Put your hands behind your back, put your hands behind your back, put your hands behind your back. Put your hands behind your back. Put your hands behind your back.

Look out.

Get down.

Take him down.

NOW.

All of this is the sum and substance of what the enhanced audio portion reveals about the officers' commands during the eighty-two seconds of the videotape. Not even a hint of racial slur can be found.

Strenuous efforts nevertheless were made by the Los Angeles District Attorney's office, and the FBI, and federal prosecutors to discover racial bigotry on the audio portion of the tape. But it was no good—not the slightest indication of racial bias emerged in the officers' handling of the arrest.

And that is why the federal government, in asking for indictments against the officers, *specifically rejected race as a motivating factor in either the arrest or the charges ultimately leveled against Koon and the other officers.* You can bet a month's salary that with racial tensions running so high, any evidence that could be uncovered would have been used either at the Simi Valley trial or the subsequent federal proceedings.

Given all of this, you would assume that race would not have been a factor. But just as the spirit of the law had little if anything to do with the prosecution of Koon and his fellow officers, so reason played no part in the proceedings. The issue was political. Specifically, racial politics had been put into play. And when racial politics is raised, however subtly, reason flies out the door.

Race and Politics in Los Angeles

The arrest of Rodney King on March 3, 1991, actually began in 1982. That was when the Los Angeles Police Department, at the demands of minority and liberal members of the Police Commission and Los Angeles City Council, outlawed the chokehold as a means of subduing a resisting suspect.[10]

The chokehold is a restraint of proven effectiveness. Had the chokehold been available as an in-policy use of force by the LAPD on March 3, 1991, Rodney King would have been subdued and the incident over before the Holliday videotape had even begun.

But the practice had been outlawed almost ten years before. Minority members of the Los Angeles City Council and Police Commission had argued that it was being used too freely against black and Hispanic suspects, all too frequently with fatal results. Hence, the chokehold was an instrument of white cop repression of minorities and thus should be outlawed. Two members of the Los Angeles City Council were especially instrumental in removing the chokehold from police policy.

One was Robert Farrell, who represented a mostly black district and charged that when the chokehold was used "most of those who die... are black... and that other city leaders care little about the lives of black men." This is the same Robert Farrell who later acknowledged that eliminating the chokehold would result in more police baton beatings, à la Rodney King, but that such beatings would be more "cost effective" in settling complaints than lawsuits stemming from the chokehold. In other words, when you got right down to it, to Farrell, the issue was money, not principle.

Another LA City Council member in 1982 when the chokehold was outlawed was Zev Yaroslavsky, now a Los Angeles County supervisor. His hypocrisy on the issue is almost breathtaking. In 1982, Yaroslavsky insisted that eliminating the chokehold would cut down on lawsuit settlements. Just the "financial effects" of using the chokehold "should be a persuasive factor" for people who "are not moved by considerations of conscience or public policy," Yaroslavsky said in arguing to abandon the chokehold.

But things didn't work out exactly as planned by Farrell, Yaroslavsky, and other supporters of a chokehold ban. In fact, after the chokehold was eliminated from the LAPD's tool kit successful lawsuits for excessive uses of force increased by a factor of ten.

This is important in the context of the Rodney King episode because the Los Angeles City Council, at Yaroslavsky's urging, hired an outside attorney to cut a deal with King's lawyer and reach an out-of-court settlement for damages King alleged to have sustained from the beating. The attorney offered King and his lawyer

$5.9 million. It's problematic whether the offer would have been accepted; when taken to the Los Angeles City Council for consideration, the body rejected the offer as too generous. In the end, King got $3.8 million from the city. The council believed it got a deal. King's lawyers thought they had been robbed. The only real winners were Yaroslavsky and a few other council members, who were able to hide behind the smokescreen of the settlement offer and final payment and thus conceal their own culpability in advancing a policy that led directly to the Rodney King episode.

However, the depressing reality of this sorry tale is not what happened on March 3, 1991, as a result of the Police Commission's and City Council's change of policy on acceptable uses of force. Rather, it is that everyone knew that the change of policy someday would make inevitable the Rodney King beating, or something very much like it. And they had known it for almost ten years.

As early as May 7, 1982, Captain Tom Hayes, commanding officer of the LAPD Training Division, wrote a memo about what the change of policy meant. He wrote:

> The Police Commission moratorium on the use of upper body control holds [chokeholds] has created a void in the department's use of force philosophy that seriously affects the ability of field personnel to adhere to established guidelines and function in a safe and effective manner....
>
> The current use of force "barometer" establishes stringent guidelines that are no longer applicable.

Then, almost as if he anticipated what would happen on March 3, 1991, he continued:

> *The prohibition of upper body control holds requires expansion of the use of the baton to control combative suspects. The pain compliance, blocking and striking capabilities of the PR 24 baton are far superior to the straight baton and provide uniformed officers with an effective tool when confronted with non-cooperative suspects. The use of upper body control holds are only authorized in situations when the use of deadly force is authorized* [emphasis added].

In other words, the new policy meant that cops would be forced to use their batons more often. And in the Rodney King incident, specifically, it meant that the chokehold—which Koon said would have subdued King in less than half a minute had it been available— was no different in policy from unholstering a pistol and shooting Rodney King. And that option, deadly force, was one that Koon sought to avoid in the arrest in favor of a more graduated response using minimum escalations of force, depending on Rodney King's behavior.

The Hayes memorandum, written nine years before the Rodney King episode, clearly anticipated events. Using an upper body control such as the chokehold, Hayes told LAPD management, is "only authorized in situations when the use of deadly force is authorized." The reason, he said, was that "at this level of force it would be extremely dangerous to attempt the use of an upper body control hold... [because to do so] puts an officer's weapon in jeopardy of being used against him, his partner, or any citizen in close proximity."

So the only reasonable alternative, Hayes said, was to use a PR 24 baton, which "provides a safe and viable method of handling situations where officers are faced with bodily attack by a suspect... an officer's decision to draw or exhibit a baton should be based on the officer's reasonable belief that there is a risk that the situation may escalate."

Scrapping the chokehold, Hayes warned, "would only provide less protection for the citizens of Los Angeles and would be callous disregard for police officers who must face an increasing tide of physical violence."

His 1982 memo concluded:

> Without clear direction and support from the department relative to the use of force, officers will resort to any method or technique that "gets the job done." *This type of approach would create a serious liability problem for the City, the department and the involved officers.* Unfortunately, the existing political and emotional climate [against using the chokehold] leaves little hope for a reinstitution of the upper body control holds as authorized techniques to handle combative suspects. *City management has been advised*

that the expanded use of the baton is our only alternative
[emphasis added].

In other words, city management was on notice that what did happen would happen. Given Hayes's clear warning almost a decade before, it is nothing short of dishonest for the city and LAPD management to act as though neither official body was aware of the risks involved in leaving a gaping hole in the uses of force permissible to police officers. Hayes's forebodings, moreover, were verified on several occasions prior to March 3, 1991. The difference was that on these occasions videocameras weren't on hand to capture the lapse of policy on tape.

Now, return to Hansen Dam Recreational Park on March 3, 1991. Rodney King had refused to respond to legal commands. He had resisted efforts to restrain his freedom. He had either already attacked an officer or attempted to flee. He had absorbed two TASER blasts of fifty thousand volts each.

By this time the officers had dug as deeply as they could into the bag of tricks given them by the Police Commission, the Los Angeles City Council, and police management. These official supervisory bodies had said, in effect, that the cops had no choice but to use the PR 24 baton or shoot Rodney King. Shooting is maximum force. And Koon's objective was to use minimum force.

This was a major theme of the defense at Simi Valley—the use of force was reasonable and necessary under the circumstances and well within LAPD policies, training, and procedures.

Moreover, an authoritative police witness supported the cops. The witness was Sergeant Charles Duke, a muscular bear of a man in his late forties and a longtime use-of-force training officer at the Police Academy. Duke had met Koon only once briefly before the trial and did not know any of the other officers when he agreed to testify for the defense. He brought with him credentials that included training military personnel as well as police officers in unarmed combat techniques and years of experience as a street cop.

Duke was an extremely credible witness at Simi Valley. To counter his testimony, the prosecution offered Commander Michael Bostic, a management stalwart but basically an administrative officer who had difficulty offsetting Duke's experienced contention that Koon and his officers operated well within departmental guidelines.

The state prosecution's failure to have an effective counterwitness to Sergeant Duke at Simi Valley was righted by federal prosecutors when their turn to batter the officers arrived. And just to make sure they were fully covered, federal prosecutors, working in tandem with LAPD management, did an effective job of fuzzing up LAPD policies and conveniently failing to disclose evidence that supported the officers' case.

But all of this was more than two years in the future back in March 1991. In the meantime, the state proceeded with its prosecution of the officers, and detectives from the LAPD Internal Affairs Division (IAD) continued to investigate the matter.

A couple of points about the IAD investigation need to be made in light of the subsequent federal prosecution.

First, IAD proceedings are different from what most people consider typical criminal investigations. In a routine criminal probe, a suspect is given the right to remain silent if he or she wishes. That is a basic constitutional guarantee. But when a cop is suspected of a crime, the cop is also a government employee who can be disciplined administratively without a judicial proceeding.

Accordingly, what happened was this:

The cops—Koon, Powell, Wind, and Briseno—were invited in by the IAD and told they were under investigation for using excessive force on Rodney King. They then were asked if they wished to remain silent. The cops said they did. OK, the IAD investigators said, that gets us over the criminal hump. You have a right to remain silent. Now we'll move on to the administrative part of our case. If you don't answer questions, you can be punished, even fired. Now, do you still wish to remain silent? The cops said they'd talk. It might seem a bit heavy-handed, but it's routine procedure in most cities.

Here's the further rub, though. Those administrative statements are then available in criminal proceedings. They're not supposed to be, but as a practical matter they are. The Rodney King episode was even worse because of the enormous amount of publicity it had generated. And someone—no one knows who or why—even leaked some of Koon's IAD statements to the media, where the information was reported in public. And any potential witness in a criminal trial who has access to a cop's administrative statements is supposed to be tainted by possessing that information, and thus disqualified from testifying.

So what happens when the allegedly confidential information is reported in a newspaper? And what further happens when a defendant is also a witness, like Theodore Briseno? As a codefendant with Koon, Wind, and Powell, Briseno had access to his fellow officers' accounts of the arrest of Rodney King, and he can be assumed to have read newspapers about Koon's confidential statements that were reported in the general media. As a hostile witness testifying against his fellow officers, he shouldn't have been provided access to *any* information about what the other three officers told the cops. Thus, the agonizing clash of constitutional rights: To deny Briseno the right to testify in his own behalf would violate Briseno's constitutional guarantees, yet to allow him to do so with prior knowledge of what the other officers had said to the IAD in administrative proceedings would violate their constitutional rights.

What's right, and what's wrong? There is no straightforward answer to these questions. The answers will emerge later and ultimately may vindicate Koon and Powell.

The second point about the IAD investigation is that the internal security police tried mightily to prove that a conspiracy existed among the officers to cover up the seriousness of the incident that occurred on March 3, 1991.

Yet no trace of a conspiracy was ever found. Because none existed. But in the curious logic of the IAD, the absence of proof was in itself evidence of a conspiracy. Accordingly, the LAPD handed out disciplinary punishments to all of the probationary officers present at the scene on March 3, 1991, and to some of the more senior patrol personnel. The officers who weren't indicted were accused of having failed to halt an illegal use of force.

The IAD's suspicion of a conspiracy would come back to haunt the internal security police. For when the FBI got into the case, the investigating federal agents were equally insistent that a cover-up conspiracy existed on the LAPD—and this time the IAD was on the hit list. What goes around comes around. And here again the failure to find evidence of a conspiracy was regarded as proof that one existed. The FBI wasted thousands of taxpayer dollars following up dead-end leads and groundless rumors that led nowhere. Like the racial issue, the conspiracy theory had no substance.

But the basic issue wasn't conspiracy, it was the beating of Rodney King. Under LA County District Attorney Ira Reiner, a grand jury investigation began almost immediately. The key piece of evidence was the videotape, still fresh in everyone's minds, still being broadcast on local as well as network television every time a new development of the story emerged, which was almost daily. Almost twenty LAPD officers testified before the state grand jury and all told basically the same story—that Rodney King was out of control and presented a threat and had to be physically subdued with the tools police officers were allowed to use. The grand jury did not invite Koon to testify until the night before the indictments were handed up. Koon declined the invitation, since he would be at the mercy of hostile prosecutors and vulnerable to questioning without his own attorney present.

On March 14, 1991, just eleven days after the incident, sealed indictments were issued charging Koon with assault with a deadly weapon, assault under color of authority, filing a false police report, and accessory after the fact to a felony. Powell was charged with two assault counts and one accusation of filing a false police report. Wind and Briseno were both charged with assault with a deadly weapon and assault under color of authority.

All four officers were immediately suspended (they had been placed on administrative leave earlier), and Wind, the probationer, was fired since he had not yet earned the job safety conferred by one year's tenure on the force. The date was March 15, 1991.

That was the last day any of the four ever got paid by the Los Angeles Police Department, although they were facing an ordeal that would leave them penniless. Indeed, the cost to the Los Angeles Protective League for legal representation eventually exceeded $1 million in attorney's fees. Nor was the cost of what lay ahead just financial or confined to the four officers.

Wind's health would fail; his marriage begin to disintegrate. Briseno faced the contempt of fellow officers for testifying against Koon and Powell and, to a lesser degree, Wind, at Simi Valley. Powell's tribulations, like Koon's, would include a prison term. Los Angeles Police Chief Daryl Gates would be forced to resign his position under fire from the Los Angeles City Council and Mayor Tom Bradley, Gates's longtime political enemy. District Attorney Reiner would lose his job, too. Rodney King would become a useful symbol for minority politicians to put on display whenever it served a practical purpose; as the Reverend Leonard Jackson of the First African-American Methodist Episcopal Church in Los Angeles told *Newsweek* in May 1994, Rodney King had become "if not a hero, then a vessel." Countless people's lives would be left in ruins by the riots. As some looters rampaged through Los Angeles, throwing trash cans through windows and looting stores, they shouted, "This is for Rodney King."[11]

The story of the Simi Valley trial and the Los Angeles riots that followed almost as soon as the not-guilty verdicts were rendered has been told and retold so often that nothing material can be added here. Suffice it to say that as the state prosecution proceeded, the federal government lurked in the background, following the indictment, trial, and verdict with great interest.

No one really expected the defendants to be found innocent. The media had prepared everybody for a guilty verdict. In fact, a public opinion poll sponsored by the *Los Angeles Times* and published November 16, 1992, indicated that most people in the Los Angeles area thought the news media were as responsible for the riots as the verdict.

But once the fires started, with race the central issue on everyone's minds and the Holliday videotape appearing in endless loops along with the scenes of violence, the pressure to go after Koon and his fellow officers was apparently more than the federal government could stand.

The Justice Department was at the ready to go into immediate action. All it needed was marching orders. And that message, the command, came from the very top.

V

WILLFUL INJUSTICE

Sentence first—verdict afterwards.

Lewis Carroll, 1865
Alice's Adventures in Wonderland

Preconceived Bias

Federal courthouses are stately monuments to the majesty of law. Yet these solemn structures are also hotbeds of political gossip and, sometimes, intrigue.

This should surprise no one. The law is a creature of politics and thrives within a political environment. Laws are made by politicians; two-thirds of the members of the U.S. Senate and almost half of the members of the House of Representatives are lawyers, or have legal educations, as are more than half the members of all fifty state legislatures combined. Judges are either appointed by politicians or seek election as politicians. Law and politics are inseparably mingled.

And so it was that as Los Angeles sweltered during the summer months of June and July 1992, the Edward T. Roybal Federal Building in Los Angeles bubbled with political rumors and gossip related to the grand jury investigation of whether Koon, Powell, Wind, and Briseno would be charged with federal violations of Rodney King's civil rights on March 3, 1991. Rumor-mill odds gave the officers little chance of avoiding indictments. The only questions were whether it would be possible to get indictments handed down before the November presidential election, and whether any of the sixteen other officers (not counting the helicopter cops) at the scene on March 3, 1991, would also get slugged with charges.

Two of the rumors were especially juicy.

The first involved U.S. District Attorney Lourdes Baird, a UCLA graduate (B.A., 1973; J.D., 1976), former municipal court judge for the city of Los Angeles, and appointee as U.S. district attorney by President George Bush in 1990. Baird was on the Dean's Honor List in the honors program as an undergraduate and was voted alumnus of the year at UCLA Law School in 1991.

According to courthouse gossip, Baird was promised a seat on the federal bench if a grand jury could bring in an indictment against the officers *before* Labor Day when the November election campaigns traditionally got under way. If so, then the Bush administration could rightfully proclaim that it was vigorously pursuing the Rodney King episode and thus perhaps win favor with some traditionally Democratic voters.

With her credentials, you could go farther and do worse than tapping Baird to get indictments against the four officers. That's because federal grand juries are wholly dependent upon the U.S. attorneys who guide them. They examine only those witnesses the U.S. attorney wants them to examine. They hear only the testimony the U.S. attorney wants them to hear. A suspect who appears voluntarily before a federal grand jury needs a psychiatric examination, since witnesses appear under oath and without the comforting presence of counsel at the witness table. Manipulating a grand jury into indictments is child's play for any smart U.S. attorney. If any legal proceeding can be rigged for political purposes, it's a federal grand jury indictment.[1] And a federal grand jury indictment of the Foothill Four officers would have considerable political payoffs, certainly in the minority community.

The rumor of a federal judgeship in return for early indictments is typical of courthouse gossip—mindless speculation and nothing more. No evidence existed then or now that such a promise was made by President Bush or anyone close to him. Still, it's another incident of historical curiosity that the federal grand jury indictment against the officers, charges that were engineered and directed by Lourdes Baird, came down on August 4, 1992, and that eight days later, on August 12, 1992, Lourdes Baird was nominated for a lifetime tenure on the federal bench. After Senate confirmation, she was elevated to the federal judiciary on September 9, 1992.

The second rumor making the rounds at the Roybal Federal Building may not have been as politically sexy but it had more substance from a legal standpoint. It involved a memorandum, allegedly written by a senior official of the Justice Department, that said, in effect, get indictments and convictions against these officers and do whatever it takes to get them. And, by the way, get it done before the November election if you can. Indeed, the rumor was so pervasive that it aired in the national media.

On November 30, 1992, three months before the officers' trial began at the Roybal courthouse, *Newsweek* reported that "a critical inside memo" had been leaked to Michael P. Stone, Powell's attorney. According to the magazine, Justice Department officials were "fuming over the leak—and determined to find out who's to blame."

That a secret memorandum of some importance existed is not at issue. But no one in a position to know what the memo said specifically can talk about it without risking contempt-of-court charges. What is known is this: Stone received a confidential government document that had been mailed to him, presumably by accident. Stone dutifully (some defense sympathizers used the word "stupidly," although that's not altogether fair since as an attorney Stone is an officer of the court and thus bound by law to play by the rules) returned it to government prosecutors through Judge Davies. Apparently inflammatory, the memorandum was immediately placed under seal at the request of prosecutors without even Judge Davies having read it. And there the government memorandum remains, under court seal, unavailable to anyone seeking proof of whether the government acted with conscious, premeditated malice in prosecuting Koon, Powell, Wind, and Briseno a second time.

But such secondary proof of prosecutorial intent is really unnecessary. The vengeful objective of the federal government, with all of the vast muscle it could bring to bear against Koon and his colleagues, had already been made public. And it had been made public by no less an authority than the president of the United States, George Bush.

On May 1, 1992, as Los Angeles continued to burn, President Bush issued one of the most remarkable statements about a criminal court case ever to emanate from the White House. It suggested preconceived notions of guilt despite earlier evidence of innocence. It was a scorn of personal rights with few precedents in presidential history.

Bush's comments at a May 1, 1992, press conference all but convicted Koon, Powell, Wind, and Briseno, and virtually guaranteed that they would be unable to receive a fair trial anywhere in the United States, certainly not in Los Angeles where the flames were still burning. If marching orders for the Justice Department ever existed, the presidential press conference provided unmistakable proof of what the federal government intended to do in the case—regardless of the first trial's verdict and despite at least two, perhaps three, sections of the Bill of Rights that ought to have protected the police officers from a government bent on spiteful revenge.

Fully half of Bush's prepared remarks on the federal government's response to the Los Angeles riots was devoted to the Simi Valley verdict. Since the president's statements were so strong and set the tone for the Justice Department's actions over the next several months, they are worth repeating at some length here. After describing what the government was doing to quell the civil disorders in Los Angeles, the president said:

> And now let's talk about the beating of Rodney King, because beyond the urgent need to restore order is the second issue, the question of justice, whether Rodney King's federal civil rights were violated. What you saw and what I saw in the [Holliday] TV video was revolting. I felt anger. I felt pain. I thought, "How can I explain this to my grandchildren?"
>
> Civil rights leaders, and just plain citizens fearful of and sometimes victimized by police brutality, were deeply

hurt. And I know good and decent policemen who were equally appalled.

I spoke this morning to many leaders of the civil rights community. And they saw the video, as we all did. For fourteen months they waited patiently, hopefully. They waited for the system to work. And when the verdict came in, they felt betrayed. Viewed from outside the trial, it was hard to understand how the verdict could possibly square with the video. Those civil rights leaders with whom I met were stunned, and so were my kids. But the [innocent] verdict Wednesday was not the end of the process.

The Department of Justice had started its own investigation immediately after the Rodney King incident and was monitoring the state investigation and trial. And so let me tell you what actions we are taking at the federal level to ensure that justice is served.

Within one hour of the verdict, I directed the Justice Department to move into high gear on its own independent criminal investigation into the case.

And next, on Thursday, five federal prosecutors were on their way to Los Angeles. Our Justice Department has consistently demonstrated its ability to investigate fully a matter like this. Since 1988,[2] the Justice Department has successfully prosecuted over one hundred law enforcement officials for excessive violence. I'm confident that in this case the Department of Justice will act as it should.

Federal grand jury action is under way in Los Angeles. Subpoenas are being issued. Evidence is being reviewed. The federal effort in this case will be expeditious, and it will be fair. It will not be driven by mob violence, but by respect for due process and the rule of law.

We owe it to Americans who put their faith in the law to see that justice is served. But as we move forward on this or any other case, we must remember the fundamental tenet of [our] legal system: Every American, whether accused or accuser, is entitled to protection of his or her rights.

In this controversial court case a verdict was handed down by a California jury. To Americans of all races who were shocked by the verdict, let me say this: You must understand that our system of justice provides for the peaceful, orderly means of addressing this frustration. We must respect the process of law, whether or not we agree with the outcome.

President Bush's comments merit examination, "parsing," because of the clear impact they had in getting the cops behind bars.

The president said, "What you saw and what I saw in the TV video was revolting. I felt anger. I felt pain. I thought, 'How can I explain this to my grandchildren?'"

What the president saw on the video was indeed revolting. It did generate pain and anger. It was brutal, it was ugly. But it also was and is a harsh reality of police life of the streets that sometimes a law-breaker won't obey legal commands to be taken into custody. Most people saw the ugly section of the videotape. What they didn't see were all of the preceding efforts the police officers had made to subdue King peacefully. What they didn't see were Rodney King's repeated aggressions, his attempts to rise and resist being taken into custody.

What were the cops' options? The police officers followed the rules—they subdued King in accordance with LAPD policies for taking combative suspects into custody. Should they have shot him instead? Would deadly force have generated any less anger and pain? After all, once Rodney King was stopped he had to be taken into custody, however much he resisted; to do otherwise would have violated the law. Wouldn't it be more appropriate to explain to grandchildren the importance of law and order rather than the supremacy of political expediency?

The point is this: The president's remarks were a clear indication that he believed the cops were guilty, regardless of evidence heard by the Simi Valley jury. His belief in the policemen's guilt was apparently based on ignorance of the facts. Either that, or it was rooted in a deliberate, calculated rejection of any evidence of the cops' innocence in a cynical attempt to stroke the "many leaders of the civil rights community" he had spoken with before the press conference.

The president said, "Viewed from outside the trial, it was hard to understand how the verdict could possibly square with the video. Those civil rights leaders with whom I met were stunned, and so were my kids."

Well, of course that's true—"viewed from outside the trial." The media had prepared the public all too well for a guilty verdict with the edited Holliday videotape. But the Simi Valley jury saw the entire videotape and heard a version of the incident that was very different from the one being aired in the media. The jury saw the video frame by frame in slow motion, again and again, and it clearly revealed Rodney King's aggressive behavior—behavior that even the federal judge and federal jury acknowledged was basically responsible for the incident.

Perhaps the "civil rights leaders" with whom President Bush met were "stunned." After all, they had a vested interest in a guilty verdict, which would have validated all of the racially based criticisms of the LAPD that had been leveled by them over the years. The fact is that civil rights leaders believed that in the Holliday videotape they had slam-dunk evidence for which there was no explanation save racial bias. But President Bush's kids? They presumably would be more impartial than their politically motivated father and the civil rights leaders he was wooing in a presidential election year.

The president said, "The Department of Justice had started its own investigation immediately after the Rodney King incident and was monitoring the state investigation and trial. And so let me tell you what actions we are taking at the federal level to ensure that justice is served. Within one hour of the verdict, I directed the Justice Department to move into high gear on its own independent criminal investigation into the case. And next, on Thursday [the day after the verdicts], five federal prosecutors were on their way to Los Angeles."

This is an important point, one that is related to the issue of double jeopardy (which will be discussed in more detail in the section of chapter VI entitled *A Victory for the Defense*). The president acknowledged that the federal government had begun its investigation in tandem with the state, and "was monitoring the state investigation and trial." In short, the federal government had at its command not only the Simi Valley trial record, which was public, but also all of the state's investigative findings, many of which were not public.

One test of whether the officers' double jeopardy protection has been violated is whether the state and federal authorities openly cooperated in dual prosecutions. If the state and federal governments cooperated, then a defendant's Fifth Amendment rights possibly—maybe even likely—have been violated. Perhaps "monitoring" the state proceedings doesn't fit a dictionary definition of cooperation, but it comes perilously close. After the Simi Valley trial, the government had at its command all the facts accumulated by the state prosecution, all witness testimony, and a road map for the defense strategy at the second trial. If not *de jure* double jeopardy, this at least constitutes *de facto* intrusion upon if not deprivation of Fifth Amendment protection against dual prosecution.

The president said, "Our Justice Department has consistently demonstrated its ability to investigate fully a matter like this. Since 1988, the Justice Department has successfully prosecuted over one hundred law enforcement officials for excessive violence. I'm confident that in this case the Department of Justice will act as it should."

If an example of prejudgment conviction ever existed, this is it: the president of the United States, on national television, talking about successful prosecution of law enforcement officials for "excessive violence" and expressing confidence that "the Department of Justice will act as it should." At no time did he even hint that the officers might be innocent, that the evidence was contradictory, that Rodney King was a felony evader. It was just the officers, guilty as ordained by the media and political opportunists even if not by the recent panel of jurors.

Clearly neither truth nor justice ruled that day. Given such a command by the president, if a bureaucrat valued his or her job, and if he or she was driven by the situational ethics that propel politics, the obvious inference was to go after the officers with all of the powers in the government's arsenal. And that's just what the Department of Justice did.

So, you see, in the final analysis, the validity of the rumors was really unimportant. It was unimportant whether the attorney general of the United States or one of the attorney general's principal functionaries transmitted an instruction that the cops should be tried and convicted post haste. It was unimportant that Lourdes Baird got a federal judgeship.

It was all unimportant because the political climate for prosecution had already been established on national television by the president of the United States. And so the Justice Department troops in Washington hastily packed their bags and booked transportation to Los Angeles.

As a postscript to the president's May 1 message, one other statement made by the nation's chief magistrate is also worth repeating because, unlike the marching orders, it was blatantly ignored by the Justice Department prosecutors. "The federal effort in this case will be expeditious, and it will be fair," President Bush said. "It will not be driven by mob violence, but by respect for due process and the rule of law."

Precisely the opposite happened. The federal case, however expeditious, certainly was unfair. And, in a sense, it was driven by mob violence—the fear of another LA riot. The federal process, moreover, was propelled by casual contempt for "due process and the rule of law."

The ruthless abuse of official power was about to begin. And it was initiated by the president of the United States.

Official Intimidation

President Bush was technically accurate in stating that only five federal prosecutors from Washington had been transferred to Los Angeles to lead the effort to indict and convict the Foothill Four.

But this number didn't include the additional Washington-based Justice Department attorneys, FBI agents, and other investigators experienced in civil rights matters who also were assigned to the task force. With these frontline troops added to the Los Angeles-based prosecution staff and FBI office, you get a better idea of the resources the government was able to muster against the four officers. Within days the total strength of the government forces reached more than sixty. It was a formidable force of manpower, brainpower, legal talent, and money. To give you an idea of just what the case cost taxpayers, the government reported to Koon's lawyer after the trial that it had accumulated fully 260,000 separate pieces of paper—which would make a stack about eighty-six feet tall—on Koon alone. The ultimate cost of the investigation and prosecution would exceed $1 million.

Leading this small army was the Justice Department's premier civil rights prosecutor, Barry Kowalski, a career civil servant and deputy section chief for the Justice Department's Civil Rights Division in Washington and special counsel of its Criminal Section. An affable, engaging man whose kind demeanor conceals the tough former Marine officer he was (a platoon leader during the Vietnam War), the forty-eight-year-old Kowalski had been a key figure in several high-profile government cases involving civil rights violations, from white supremacist terror groups in the Pacific Northwest and Rocky Mountains to Confederate Hammerhead skinheads in Dallas.

Kowalski's lead assistant was Steven Clymer, a senior prosecutor in the Los Angeles U.S. Attorney's office. A Cleveland native and graduate of Cornell University and Cornell Law School, Clymer had almost ten years' experience arguing government cases, first as an assistant district attorney in Philadelphia and, since 1987, as an assistant U.S. attorney in Los Angeles. Clymer enjoys a reputation as a first-rate prosecutor, maybe not in Kowalski's major-league category but certainly as a triple-A contender.

From the beginning, the course of the investigation was set to strengthen a case whose weaknesses had been exposed by the Simi Valley verdict of not guilty. Among other things, this meant, if possible, finding evidence that racial bias influenced the officers' actions; that the officers conspired to cover up the seriousness of the offense; and that the "swarm" technique was an approved LAPD policy that the officers had ignored in favor of using PR 24 batons to beat up on Rodney King. This last objective was critical, because it would demonstrate that the officers *wanted* to beat Rodney King rather than simply to subdue him.

One way to accomplish these ends would be to get some of the officers to change or alter their testimony given either to the state grand jury that brought the first charges against Koon et al. or at the Simi Valley trial. And one way to do this would be to badger certain officers into altering or withdrawing their earlier statements.

"Badger" is a polite way of saying "intimidate."

Consider, for example, the experience of Sergeant Robert Troutt. Now retired, Troutt had been the watch commander at the Valley Traffic Division when Powell asked for off-site booking approval to lodge a felony evasion charge against King. Troutt's testimony was important because it rebutted prosecution witnesses who suggested that the procedure was requested as part of a police conspiracy to cover up the seriousness of the incident.

On May 5, 1992, at 7:00 P.M. Troutt was on duty at the Devonshire Station when he received notification that an FBI agent and Justice Department attorney wanted to meet with him at 8:00 P.M. to conduct an interview. Troutt tried to get an attorney from the Police Protective League (the LAPD union for officers with the rank of lieutenant and below) to attend the meeting with him, but given the late hour and brief notice was unable to do so.

At 8:10 P.M. Special Agent David S. Park of the FBI and Department of Justice trial attorney Suzanne K. Drouet arrived at the station.

"I told them that I had spoken with the Protective League and did not wish to speak with them until I contacted an attorney. Drouet told me that their discussion with me would be informal… and that I would not need an attorney," Troutt later said in an affidavit. Thus

> due to their persistence I invited both of them to walk into the area office of [the] Devonshire Station. Captain Ken Small was in his office. I walked into his office and explained the situation to him and asked him if we could use his office. I also requested that he [Captain Small] sit in on the interview. He told me he would be glad to do so….
>
> Drouet told me that she just wanted to know general information, such as my rank, how long I've been in law enforcement, etc. I responded in words to the effect that most of that information would be on the transcript from my testimony in Simi Valley. She replied in a disgusted manner that she did not have those transcripts with her. She also asked me if I was nervous about something.
>
> I replied that I certainly was nervous about the entire incident since it is foremost in the President of the United States mind [sic] all the way down to the everyday

citizen. Drouet responded with words to the effect, "Well, *maybe there is more to your involvement than I thought, I thought we might be able to conduct this interview this way instead of having you testify before the grand jury*" [emphasis added].

I again told them that I did not wish to discuss the incident prior to speaking with an attorney. I told them it was my intention to cooperate with them in every way, but that I wanted to exercise my constitutional rights.

It appeared to me that as the above conversation progressed, Drouet became more and more rude and intimidating in her approach to me. I certainly did not feel comfortable and wanted the interview to cease until I had the chance to speak with an attorney....

I sure was glad that Captain Small had sat in during the above interview, because [on the same evening] at 10:25 PM [Devonshire] Lieutenant Jackson received a phone call from Barry Kowalski, Deputy Chief of the Civil Rights Division.... The note written by Lieutenant Jackson at the time of his conversation with Kowalski stated, "Kowalski wants Sergeant Troutt in his office Friday morning at 10 AM and may bring an attorney. He stated Troutt was rude and uncooperative and wouldn't tell [Drouet] what his position with the [Police] Department is."

On the advice of his League-sponsored attorney, Diane Marchandt, Troutt declined to meet with Kowalski. Troutt later testified for the defense at the federal criminal trial, saying essentially the same thing he said at Simi Valley—that the booking procedure used in the Rodney King incident was entirely proper according to departmental procedures.

Troutt's experience was one of the mildest of the attempts made to intimidate witnesses who might be helpful to the defense or harmful to the prosecution. Diane Marchandt, attorney for the Police Protective League, recalls two in particular.

"One FBI agent was interviewing an officer who worked at Foothill [Division]," Marchandt said.[3] "This was at a time when the U.S. Attorney's office was trying to dig up evidence that Larry

Powell had used excessive force in the past, although everybody knew that acts of prior misconduct would not be admissible in the trial....[4]

"And one [FBI] agent in particular... couldn't get the officer to say what he wanted him to say, and so he asked the officer, 'Do you have any children?'

"And the officer said, 'No, I don't.'

"And so the FBI agent said, 'Well, I have a little boy, and he really likes to play with my badge because it's bright and shiny and sometimes when I watch him play with my badge I think, I sure wouldn't want anything to happen to my badge.'

"Was that intimidating? Sure it was," Marchandt continued—suggesting, as it did, that if the officer didn't play ball he'd lose his job.

"At that point we really got angry. He [the FBI agent] began threatening the officer with a federal statute that makes it a crime to lie to a federal agent. And so we just stood up and I asked, 'Are we under arrest?' And he said, 'No, you're not.' So we left.

"And we ran into Clymer and Kowalski right outside the door and I said, 'Don't even speak to me. We're angry. We're leaving.' And the very next morning the first thing I did was to call the [LAPD] chief of police and let him know we'd walked out of an interview, because I knew that the officer could be in trouble for not cooperating. And, of course, we weren't permitted to tape-record the interview, and the FBI doesn't take notes, because notes are discoverable as evidence.

"Anyway, when I got through to the chief's office I reported that we'd walked out of an interview and I wanted the chief to know what we'd done and why. He said he already knew about it." To Marchandt, it clearly indicated that federal prosecutors and LAPD senior managers were working closely together during the federal investigation.

Another police witness, one Marchandt described as "unimportant" to the Rodney King episode, "had not been real cooperative" with FBI agents trying to interview him.

"I called him from the U.S. Attorney's office and told him not to feel picked on, that a lot of other officers had been subpoenaed, and that I'd be with him and everything would be OK," Marchandt recalled.

"He finally agreed to accept the grand jury subpoena and gave me his home address. So I gave his address to the agent and said he's willing to accept service [of the subpoena], here's where he lives. And they [FBI agents] went out to the officer's house and knocked on the door, and he apparently didn't come to the door right away—he told me he'd been in the shower and couldn't hear anyone knocking—and when he didn't come to the door right away the federal agents disconnected his electricity to force him to come to the door."

This kind of thing, however much it might seem to emulate Inspector Clouseau's Pink Panther pranks, is small stuff. The intimidation was about to get serious. This is how it really worked.

One standard technique used by the FBI (and the LAPD Internal Affairs Division) is to begin an investigation by going after younger officers who have less experience than more senior cops. As a rule, younger officers are more vulnerable because they are still naïve enough to believe that they're the good guys and the justice system only goes after the bad guys. So if you honestly believe you've done nothing wrong, it's startling and unsettling to realize that suddenly you're a suspect. You're thrown off balance.

Consider the experience of Officer Susan Clemmer as an example.

The night of March 3, 1991, Clemmer had been on the Los Angeles police force for one year, six months, and five days. She was not even a full week into her post-probationary service. A college graduate, she had acquired a certain sophistication growing up in Wisconsin, Texas, and finally California. But she still was just twenty-three years old the night Rodney King was arrested.

Clemmer's testimony was important. She had been on patrol March 3, 1991, and was in the fourth LAPD patrol car—behind Powell and Wind, Koon's supervisory black-and-white, and the cruiser carrying Briseno and Solano—to arrive at the scene as the arrest was going down. Once Rodney King was subdued and handcuffed, Koon assigned Clemmer and Wind to ride in the ambulance with King as he was being taken to Pacifica Hospital for diagnosis and emergency treatment.

An articulate and obviously bright woman, Clemmer made a good witness. She testified at Simi Valley that during the ambulance ride King kept spitting on her uniform trousers and repeating over and over, "Fuck you, fuck you."

Once at the hospital, Clemmer testified that King's behavior continued to be bizarre; at one point, she reported, King turned to

Koon and said to the sergeant, "I love you." It was a curious, jarring statement, one that suggested a substance problem beyond simple alcohol intoxication.

If Clemmer's testimony could be shaken, one pothole in the prosecution's case would be filled, at least partially. Rodney King would not so easily be portrayed as a dangerous felony suspect who had been acting in a violent and resistant fashion, as if strung out on a controlled substance such as PCP that encourages aggressive behavior far more powerfully than alcohol or any other legal drug.

When Clemmer arrived to testify before the federal grand jury, she said she was met by two FBI agents, one male and one female. The male agent, she said, commented on the civilian suit she was wearing, remarking in a complimentary tone that it was the same one she'd worn during testimony at the Simi Valley trial and that it looked good on her. "I thought that was unusual, that he already knew so much about me that my wardrobe was included," she said.

"Then I met in a room in the U.S. Attorney's office with Kowalski, Clymer, and two other assistant U.S. attorneys," she continued. "Now the tone became definitely accusatory. Their tones were rough. They accused me of being part of a conspiracy and of lying at the state trial."

"Keep in mind that I'm very young and inexperienced," she said. "Only Kowalski and I were walking down the hall, there were no other witnesses, and he [Kowalski] said he had a daughter my age and if she lied the way you're lying now I'd disown her. He was very sarcastic; he said, 'I'm sure your parents are proud of you now.'

"And then he said it would cost my parents $5,000 to get me out of jail on bail for a conspiracy charge. I was very young, very scared. And I really believed that when I left the grand jury room it would be in handcuffs and headed for jail."

Kowalski declined to comment on Clemmer's recollection of the incident. He said federal laws prohibited him from talking about anything that occurred either inside or outside the grand jury room.

At the federal trial, Clemmer did not change her testimony about Rodney King's behavior on March 3, 1991.

Another rookie officer who testified the same day Clemmer appeared was Solano, a twenty-six-year-old Los Angeles native and college graduate with a degree in business administration.

Solano was a probationer riding with Briseno on March 3, 1991, and a witness to the entire incident once the pursuit ended. He was another witness whose testimony, if it could be cracked, would be useful to the prosecution. Although Solano had only about six months' street experience on March 3, 1991, and had said at Simi Valley that he thought that although Koon "could have handled [the arrest] better," the uses of force he witnessed—except for the team take-down—were consistent with what he had been taught at the police academy. Here's what he said in an interview about witness intimidation by the prosecution team.

> They use the good-cop, bad-cop technique. You know how it works, but you're never really prepared for it. They try to get the probationers right away. As a probationer you're not used to testifying. You're more malleable.
>
> Then when you show up for [grand jury] testimony they'll sit you down with an FBI agent and you make small talk. Then they take you into the first set of attorneys. They're called the "clean team." They take basic information that's intended to make you comfortable. If you're a male officer, they'll have a female U.S. attorney and FBI agent there taking notes. If you're a female officer, they'll have a handsome young FBI guy and an older male U.S. attorney with you. They take basic information—how many times you've testified about this matter, that sort of thing. Basically, it lulls you into a sense of, "OK, OK, this isn't going to be that bad."
>
> Then just before they put you on [the witness stand] you go and meet with one of the prosecuting attorneys. What they would do when you sit down with them, they'd tell you right up front, "Oh, we think you're a nice guy. But we know you're lying."
>
> Now, here's the thing: It's on federal property and you're not allowed to have any type of recording device that might prove what they say to you. At least with the state and [LAPD] Internal Affairs you're allowed to have a tape recorder for the interview. But not with the FBI.
>
> They say, "We think you're lying, I know you're lying,

you're lying." And after this interview you're starting to get a little bit rattled.

Here, this guy's a federal prosecutor and he's calling me a liar. You can take offense at it, but at the same time you wonder what kind of game he's going to play with you. And that's when I saw Susan Clemmer come off the stand and out the door of the grand jury room and she was visibly upset, almost in tears or maybe just finished crying, and I'm thinking, Gee, what did they do to her in there?

Then they called me in and put me on the stand and their first question was, "Officer Solano, are you aware of what perjury is? Are you aware that perjury is a federal crime punishable by up to five years in prison and a $250,000 fine?"

At that time, I thought, well, if I didn't before I certainly do now.

Solano appeared twice before the grand jury. The second time, he says, prosecutors "were still accusatory but they had toned down the rhetoric some." Altogether, before the trial began, Solano met "about five to eight" times with Kowalski and Clymer. Also present was his attorney, Diane Marchandt. The federal prosecutors never deviated from the "good-cop, bad-cop" routine, Solano says. "In some cases [with other officers] Clymer was the good guy," Solano recalled. "But with me he always played hardball and Kowalski was kind of quiet.

"The last session [before the trial began] they told me, 'Well, your memory isn't consistent with the [Holliday] videotape.'

"And I said 'I know that, I don't disagree with the tape, but I'm just telling you guys how I remember things.'

"And they said, 'OK, when we put you on the stand I can do one of two things. I can put on the tape and embarrass you, or I can just ask you a couple of questions.' And I told Diane Marchandt right then that he's going to use the tape in the trial. And that's exactly what happened.

"He [Clymer] wanted to use the tape to try to impeach me, to prove a conspiracy. But Judge Davies wouldn't let them show the tape while I was testifying."

Intimidation. It doesn't always work. But the government hadn't yet gotten to the bottom of its bag of tricks. Other tools were still available. If one didn't work, they'd just try another.

Manipulating Evidence

Just as prosecutors failed to poke holes in the testimony of any of the key defense witnesses such as Clemmer and Solano, so too did they fail to produce even a hint of evidence that racial bias played a role in the arrest of Rodney King.

As it turned out, the only trial witness to raise the racial issue directly was Rodney King. And even he began to waffle on whether the officers called him "nigger" or "killer."

And King of course was an admitted liar who had changed his story several times. He may have been a minority victim poster child for the media and civil rights groups, a witness whose quiet demeanor on the witness stand stood in sharp contrast to the defense picture of a hulking monster on March 3, 1991. But he was a liar nonetheless, and post-trial interviews with jurors indicated that his presence contributed little if anything to the prosecution case.

Granted, the controversial radio transmission by Powell, who, after answering a domestic dispute involving a black household, alluded to the incident as being "right out of Gorillas in the Mist"— presumably referring to the title of a movie about Africa. Granted, too, that the implications had obvious racist overtones.

But it was not made in the context of the Rodney King affair and thus was wholly unrelated to the events of March 3, 1991, the events under consideration. Remember, too, that Powell was not in on the start of the pursuit of Rodney King and once at the scene did not initiate any use of force but merely followed Koon's commands. Larry Powell may be a bigot, or he may have been just racially insensitive in transmitting the "Gorillas in the Mist" message. Either way, it had no bearing on the Rodney King episode.

Moreover, the indictments sought by Baird, Clymer, and Kowalski specifically omitted any charge of racial bias.[5] In fact, in announcing the indictments on August 5, 1992, U.S. Attorney Lourdes Baird went out of her way to state that race was not a factor. "As far as a racial motivation, that is not a part of these charges and we are not making that allegation," she said. Because, you see, had racial bias been a key element that required proof for conviction, the government would have lost the case in a heartbeat.

This reveals the immense, almost cosmic scope of the government's hypocrisy in prosecuting the officers: To suggest as the government did that race was not the motivating factor underlying the Justice Department's prosecution is a distortion of reality of monstrous proportions. Racial politics was the root, stem, stalk, twig, and leaf of the matter. Yet only by ignoring this vital, central element could the government hope to get indictments and convictions.

Not everyone in the media was deceived by the charade. Samuel Francis wrote in a legal column in the *Denver Post* on August 16, 1992: "The Los Angeles trial is not about fairness, constitutionality, justice or truth. It is as much a political trial as ever occupied a Soviet courtroom, and Americans need to watch a little more closely this time. The next time, it may be they who find themselves in the prisoner's dock, with virtually the whole nation as their judges."

If race was not a factor, then, why did the government go to such lengths to prove that it was?

The prosecutors, for example, asked for and got a warrant to search for and seize a document Koon had written. The document, falsely described as a manuscript, reportedly referred to King's physical actions toward CHP Officer Melanie Singer as being "Mandingo"-like. "Mandingo" refers to an African tribe, and it was the title of a novel and book of the 1950s about slavery and interracial sex. Additionally, news accounts reported that Koon had written that police officers had joked about using force against minorities. Contents of the "manuscript"—a disjointed collection of notes written as a therapeutic exercise—were presumably evidence of racial bias.[6]

Or so the prosecutors thought. As it was, prosecutors, defense attorneys, and Judge Davies gnawed at length on the meaning of "Mandingo." Judge Davies finally threw up his hands and said, enough, it's not going to be allowed into evidence since we can't even agree on a definition of "Mandingo," and anyway we're not exploring racial motivation as a reason for the alleged offense.

(Incidentally, the warrant used by the FBI seized not only the manuscript but also word-processing disks and the word processor required to read the disks. The word processor, which cost several hundred dollars, was not included in the warrant and was returned to Koon's wife only after a court order was issued demanding its return.)

In another, more serious example of trying to prove racist behavior by the cops, the FBI took the audio portion of the Holliday videotape to a sound enhancement lab to isolate the voice band and try to prove that the officers had, indeed, used the word "nigger" or some other racial slur while subduing King. But when the tape was handed back to the FBI agent and he was told that no such words existed on the recording, the agent (who happened to be African American) was so angered by the lack of racially incriminating evidence that he hurled the tape across the room, damaging a piece of lab equipment, according to investigating reports of the incident.

This second incident involving the videotape was not reported to the defense by the prosecution. It was uncovered by the defense attorneys through a third party. Failing to share this type of information with the defense tiptoes close to a violation of the Brady rule of federal evidence.

The Brady rule, named for the case from which it stemmed, requires prosecutors to provide defendants with any evidence they discover that tends to support a plea of innocence.

The reason for the Brady rule is obvious. The government is supposed to search for justice. To hide evidence suggesting or proving the innocence of a defendant is a treacherous act that undermines the fair administration of the law.

Of course, a good argument can be made that failing to provide the results of the audio analysis was not a technical violation of the Brady rule, since race was not charged in the government's indictment.

But this instance was not the only one. A more obvious instance of withholding information to which the defense was legally entitled involved a witness named Edward Nowicki, one of the nation's foremost experts on police use of force.

Ed Nowicki is a former Chicago cop—he rose from the rank of patrolman to lieutenant in less than a decade—with almost thirty years' experience in law enforcement. During his time on the streets he survived six separate shooting incidents. He has been chief of police in a small Wisconsin community, is a former municipal judge, and has a bachelor's degree in criminal justice and a master's degree in management. He is a college-level police education instructor and has trained thousands of U.S. Marines and hundreds of Navy Seals in unarmed combat techniques, in addition to educating police constabulary instructors from England, Scotland, and Wales. Nowicki is also host of a nationally syndicated radio talk show, "American Crime Line with Ed Nowicki."

All of which explains why government prosecutors sought him out as a potential witness to offset testimony on the officers' behalf from Sergeant Charles Duke of the LAPD, who had been so persuasive for the defense at Simi Valley.

When Nowicki got a call from Barry Kowalski asking if he, Nowicki, would be willing to consider testifying as an expert government witness, Nowicki said he'd be happy, even eager to do so.

"When I saw the videotape I thought the officers were criminal," Nowicki said in an interview.[7] "I thought this was an obvious case of brutality and racism. That was what I thought based on what I saw. I was in shock. I was outraged. I spoke out publicly against what I saw. And I condemned these officers. I had nothing in mind except that I'm totally convinced that these guys are criminals. It was cemented in my brain. It was locked in my thinking because of the videotape."

When Kowalski called, Nowicki said, "I told him what I thought— racist brutality by cops. And he asked, 'Would you be willing to testify, would you be willing to be an expert witness [for the government] on the use of force?' I had been judicially qualified in a number of courts as a use-of-force expert, and I said, 'Absolutely.'"

Then, Nowicki recalled, "He [Kowalski] said, 'We're willing to pay you.'

"And I said this isn't a matter of money—it's a matter of doing what's right. I'd be glad to do anything to see that criminals who wear badges and uniforms are placed in their professional coffins." All Nowicki wanted was a coach-class airplane ticket.

According to Nowicki, Kowalski said someone from the U.S. Attorney's office would be in contact to ask a few questions about whether Nowicki could qualify as a disinterested and objective expert. Shortly thereafter Nowicki received a telephone call from a government lawyer asking whether the former Chicago cop was familiar with the Christopher Commission[8] report alleging widespread racism on the LAPD, or if Nowicki had "read any compelled statements pertaining to the officers." Nowicki replied that no, "All my information came pretty much from the media."[9]

And so, on October 1, 1992, Nowicki flew to Los Angeles for a 1:30 P.M. meeting with the federal prosecution team. Now let Nowicki tell the story of what happened in his own words:

> When I got there Mr. Kowalski was real friendly. He greeted me, shook my hand, and arranged to get me some coffee. Then he sat me in a room and gave me some documents to read.
>
> And I'm starting to read some stuff about LAPD policies and training bulletins, stuff I'd never seen before and that I didn't know about.
>
> Then he [Kowalski] brought me into another room, and Mr. Clymer was there along with about ten to twelve other individuals who were either FBI agents or assistant U.S. attorneys or paralegals.
>
> And they sat me down and they showed me a videotape [the unedited version] that I never saw before.
>
> He tells me to assume a set of circumstances. He tells me about the chase—and I never knew all of this. My perception had been that this was an embarrassment to the law enforcement profession. But he's telling me about a chase, and I never knew about a chase. The media's been saying "speeding motorist." I had thought they had stopped some speeding black guy and just beat the shit out of him for being black. That was my impression.
>
> Then they tell about him [Rodney King] going on in the car, that he wouldn't pull over. And I never knew all of this. And then they said, assume the following: There were two other people in the car. I never knew there were two other people. They [Allen and Helms] got out of the car with little incident; one might have gotten pushed in the head with a flashlight. Not hit, but pushed.
>
> And they're telling me all of this, and I'm thinking Holey Moley, I didn't know this.
>
> And then they tell me that King finally gets out of the car, he does a little dance. And Melanie Singer gets out of her car with a gun in her hand. They're telling me this, and I didn't know any of it. After King gets out of his car,

two officers get on his shoulders, two on his legs. He knocks
four officers off his back. And I'm thinking, I didn't know
any of this!

So, after seeing the complete videotape and hearing the
prosecution's own account of the incident, Nowicki politely declined
to participate as an expert witness for the prosecution. He said,
"After seeing this [entire videotape]—and I can't believe what I'm
seeing, what I'm hearing them tell me—and I tell them, I can't say if
it's unreasonable force. I just can't tell. I'm looking at it, and I just
don't know. When it's finished, I tell them I cannot say it's excessive
force. I had my eyes opened up."

Earlier, Kowalski had shown Nowicki a menu from a Polish restaurant and said that after they'd done business they could have a
pleasant lunch with ethnic food they both enjoyed. But after getting
his reaction, Nowicki said, "They can't push me out the door fast
enough. And when I got on the airplane I started getting mad. I
thought, this is bullshit. And I got back home and wrote a letter to
Barry Kowalski."

In this letter, dated October 6, 1992, Nowicki wrote:

> I would like to thank you for your affording me the
> opportunity to meet with you and your staff concerning
> the possibility of using my services to give advice and/or
> testimony....
>
> Viewing the entire video, that you provided in your
> facilities in Los Angeles on October 1, 1992, was very en-
> lightening. In fact, after viewing this video I could not state
> under oath with a reasonable degree of certainty that the
> officers in the video used unreasonable or excessive force
> against Mr. Rodney King. *This opinion is based on the infor-
> mation you and your staff provided to me* coupled with my law
> enforcement and related education, training, and experi-
> ence [emphasis added].

Now, under the Brady rule the prosecution should presumably
have to share this information with the defense. Government attorneys had approached Nowicki; he had not volunteered. Based on

the prosecution's own evidence, Nowicki had developed reasonable doubts about the officers' guilt, and that's material information. But neither Kowalski nor any member of his staff informed the prosecution about Nowicki.

In the end, Nowicki did testify at the trial. But he appeared as a defense witness. Here's Nowicki's account of how it happened.

Shortly after the meeting with Kowalski, Nowicki had a chance conversation with an acquaintance, a Los Angeles lawyer. He told the lawyer about his experience with the prosecutors. The lawyer happened to be a friend of Michael Stone, Powell's attorney. So the attorney told Stone about Nowicki. Stone contacted Nowicki and asked if he'd testify for the defense.

Sure, he told Stone, I'll be happy to testify for the cops.

"I didn't think these cops were heroes, but I didn't think they were villains, either," Nowicki said. "They were just doing their job with some guy, a convicted robber who didn't want to go back to jail. Many times in my career, and I was a Chicago cop for ten years, and I was a police chief in Wisconsin, if you'd taken an isolated incident from my career and shown it out of context like the Rodney King arrest it could have looked worse than the King incident. Yeah, I'd be willing to testify for the defense."

Nowicki's story continues: Kowalski and the prosecution team made every effort to keep Nowicki from testifying. At one point, Stone called Nowicki from Judge Davies' chambers. Present, but in the background, were Judge Davies, other defense attorneys, and Kowalski and Clymer:

> Mike [Stone] said they [Kowalski and Clymer] claimed they'd shared the prosecution strategy with me and it might taint me as a witness. I said, "Mike, that's a lie." He said no, they're saying they paid you. I said, "Mike, they're liars."
>
> They're telling Judge Davies that they shared the prosecution strategy with me, that I was privy to secret information, that they paid me. They didn't pay me a single nickel. It was all lies. I got so angry. Now I'm really angry. I'm going out there to testify no matter what. Now I'm paranoid [about the government], I'm looking for people wear-

ing sunglasses and following me. But I'm going out there no matter what.

And I did. I testified. It was one of the biggest enjoyments of my professional career.

At one point Mike Stone asked, "Did you change your mind [about the officers' being guilty]?" I said yes. And he [Stone] asked me when did that happen. And I said in the office of the U.S. Attorney. And he asked who was present. And I started pointing at Mr. Barry Kowalski, Mr. Steven Clymer [and others].... I'm pointing right at them, and they're squirming in their seats. It was like being on the stand and having the lawyer ask who robbed you, and you're pointing right at the robber.

You should have seen Kowalski. I knew I had him. You should have seen his body language. He was slumped in his chair, his eyes were closed, his butt was toward the end of the chair and his legs were crossed at the ankles. And he knew and I knew, and he knew that I knew, that this was a time bomb. They got me off the stand quickly. They didn't even try to cross-examine me very much, maybe only a few minutes. Because they knew I had them, and they knew that I knew it.

A more serious potential violation of Brady rule material came with the testimony of Sergeant Mark Conta, a use-of-force expert recruited by the prosecution in another attempt to counter the testimony of Sergeant Charles Duke, who had testified for the officers at Simi Valley.

Sergeant Duke had told the jury, as Captain Tom Hayes's letter from 1982 indicated, that the team take-down approach, which never was official policy, had been abandoned as even an acceptable technique for subduing a suspect when the chokehold had been abandoned, unless lethal force was going to be applied. (And, of course, in most lethal-force cases it would hardly make sense to use a chokehold if an officer could use a pistol instead and still be operating within policy guidelines.)

This point is critical. The question most puzzled viewers of the videotape ask is this: With so many officers present at the scene, why didn't they just gang-tackle Rodney King and get him in handcuffs that way, rather than using batons to whack him into submission?

The question makes sense, but it's largely irrelevant for three reasons.

First, not all of the score of officers were present from the beginning to the end of the incident. Many responded to the call and arrived as it was being played out or as it was ending. It's unclear how many were present for most of the incident—obviously six were there, counting Solano and Clemmer in addition to the four officers on trial—but more kept arriving almost every few seconds in response to earlier radio transmissions about the chase. Koon, as the commander on the scene, was concentrating on Rodney King's behavior. He also had to keep an eye on two other suspects in the car—Allen and Helms—thus further complicating the tactical situation that was developing. So short of an emergency requiring more officers, Koon didn't have the luxury of eyeballing the scene to determine how many people he had available to handcuff King.

Second, even if the situation became more serious and he found time to look around for assistance, Koon probably would have been unable to see how many officers had arrived. Remember: He was operating in the full glare of a helicopter's blinding light—he was unable to see beyond the range of the light, and most of the officers were gathered in darkened shadows. In addition, Koon had to monitor King's behavior and actions and respond instantaneously in a rapidly developing situation that lasted less than two minutes.

Finally, and most important of all, the "swarm" simply wasn't part of LAPD policies and never had been.[10] As a fifteen-year veteran on the force, Koon had been involved in unofficial team take-downs. The team take-down was an acceptable technique, although not an approved policy. But most of the other officers—certainly Wind and Solano—had neither experience nor training in such a technique.

Yet it was crucial for the prosecution to establish as absolute fact that the "swarm" was part of the LAPD's bag of tricks and available for use in subduing an aggressive suspect. Only then could the forceful argument be made, as Sergeant Conta did, that beating Rodney King with the PR 24 baton was an unnecessary and excessive use of force. If the "swarm" was LAPD policy, federal prosecutors would have proof of intent—that the cops beat Rodney King in order to punish him. In short, if the "swarm" was policy, by not using it the cops were culpable if not guilty; if the "swarm" wasn't policy, it could be persuasively argued that whatever Koon directed the officers to do was appropriate and necessary.

Kowalski and Clymer took extreme measures to try to prove that the swarm was an integral part of use-of-force training at the police academy. According to Police Protective League attorney Diane Marchandt, Kowalski, Clymer, and FBI agents interviewed every single member of Powell's class at the police academy that could be located to find a witness to support Conta's position that the swarm must have been taught to Powell and that he didn't have to use a baton to beat Rodney King. They failed.

And they failed for the simple reason that because it was not official policy, the swarm therefore was not a part of routine instruction.

Conta testified that the swarm was taught as part of the so-called enrichment phase of academy recruit training. That's an educational euphemism. The "enrichment" portion of LAPD academy training is intended to supplement regular instruction with instruction in more exotic police techniques. In practice, though, the enrichment phase often has nothing to do with learning how to be a good street cop.

Sergeant Duke, for example, says that one day, when he was scheduled to teach the swarm to recruits during the enrichment phase, he was told to have the recruits move furniture within the police academy to accommodate a meeting of LAPD senior officers. Moving furniture was apparently higher in priority than teaching the swarm, which made a certain amount of sense since the swarm was not in any case to be used by the cops since it was not accepted, etched-in-granite policy.

The inescapable, unavoidable, and indisputable fact is that since the chokehold had been abandoned, it was simply too dangerous for one or more officers to tie up physically with a combative suspect without a sure means of subduing him—i.e., the chokehold—in addition to mere physical restraint. When a cop gets in a fistfight or a wrestling match with a suspect, that officer can lose a gun.

The LAPD recognized its own vulnerability on the swarm issue as soon as the Simi Valley trial was concluded with innocent verdicts.

Once the Los Angeles riots had been quelled, the LAPD began bus-ing officers by the hundreds back to the police academy to get train-ing in swarm techniques even though it wasn't official policy.

Indeed, even as the trial was being conducted at the Roybal Federal Building the LAPD was writing a training bulletin to incor-porate the swarm as part of its formal instruction plan. But the train-ing bulletin wasn't officially adopted and published until after the officers had been convicted and in fact not publicly issued as a policy in a widely distributed training manual until September 1995.

And here's perhaps the worst part: The officer writing the manual as the trial was under way was the very same Sergeant Mark Conta. Even as Conta testified, he knew that a training bulletin was not yet official policy, but he said nothing. An examination of his trial testi-mony shows that he carefully avoided using the word "policy" in connection with the swarm. That way, truthfulness could be main-tained (and, not coincidentally, perjury avoided) while sustaining an appearance that the swarm was an official LAPD procedure.

How important was Conta to the prosecution? Very important, according to one trial observer, a critic of the Foothill Four. "There is no doubt that both Duke and Conta carried more weight than ordinary witnesses," wrote Columbia Law School Professor George P. Fletcher.[11] "And the prosecution's countering more effectively [with Duke] than did the People's representatives in the state trial undoubtedly contributed to the jury's convicting Officer Powell and Sergeant Koon."

The prosecutors, of course, knew throughout that the training bulletin was not yet policy, but they didn't say anything about it. Similarly, the Los Angeles Police Department knew that a training bulletin was in the works, but it too was silent. About the only people who didn't know about the embryonic training bulletin were the four officers and their attorneys; they didn't learn about it until after the trial and convictions. To the prosecutors and senior com-manders of the Los Angeles Police Department, it apparently was better to sacrifice four officers than take a chance on having Koon, Powell, Briseno, and Wind again walk away free and have the city face another riot.

Thus a crucial building block in the prosecution case had a fun-damental structural flaw, clear proof that the officers were limited by a conspicuous gap in use-of-force techniques. The government attorneys were legally bound under the Brady rule to share that information with the defense—bound, of course, if real justice and truth were the goals. But justice and truth never were the objectives of the federal prosecution.

In response to a question about whether the Brady rule had been violated, Kowalski would say only that since the defense hadn't mentioned the matter in an appeal, there must have been no violation. As for Nowicki's testimony, Kowalski said no violation had occurred there either since "all the relevant material came out" during the trial. That is true. But it emerged only over the resistance of Kowalski and Clymer.

So although both federal statutes and most state criminal codes forbid the suppression of evidence that could be favorable to defendants as a violation of Fourteenth Amendment rights, the government had gotten away with actions that came perilously close to violating the Bill of Rights if not fracturing it outright.

But this case had to be won. President Bush had made that clear in his announcement of the federal investigation, and the new Clinton administration certainly wasn't going to be out-civil-righted by Republicans. This trial demanded certainty. It would be helpful if one of the officers could be turned as Briseno was at Simi Valley, even though his testimony didn't prevent a verdict of not guilty. But Briseno had no intention of testifying at the federal trial, presumably to avoid the perjury issue.

For federal prosecutors, this wasn't cause for great concern. There was a way around the problem.

The manner in which Briseno's testimony was manipulated was excellent lawyering on the part of Kowalski and his team. As noted earlier, Briseno was faced with a dilemma if he testified.

On the one hand, he could be committing perjury if he swore that he had returned to the Foothill Station immediately to report excessive force on March 3, 1991. But if he acknowledged that he hadn't returned to the station house to make such a report, he'd be weakening his own defense against the charges that he too used unreasonable force on Rodney King. So Briseno wisely exercised his Fifth Amendment right against self-incrimination and declined to take the witness stand at the federal trial.[12]

Since Briseno wouldn't testify, the question for the prosecutors was how to get his accusations against Koon, and especially Powell, before the jury. The government needed to find a crack in the defense—such as one officer blowing the whistle on his or her colleagues. To do so would also subtly implant the notion of a conspiracy among the other officers in the jury's mind, although it wasn't necessary to sustain such an accusation since it wasn't part of the federal charges. The solution the prosecutors hit upon was so simple that it should have been obvious from the start: Use Briseno's videotaped testimony at Simi Valley.

While this might appear to violate the other defendants' Sixth Amendment right to confront an accuser—how, after all, can you cross-examine a videotape?—precedent for using recorded testimony from a prior trial existed. And Judge Davies, after requiring that the tape be edited to comply with some complex and technical legal requirements, allowed the prosecution to put a videotaped Briseno on the stand and provide testimony damaging to the other officers' defense, testifying essentially *in absentia* even though Briseno was seated throughout the trial at the defense tables.

But however useful the Briseno videotaped testimony might have been for the prosecution from a purely legalistic standpoint—it did, after all, legitimize Briseno's testimony for the jury—it also contained a critical contradiction of logic. If Briseno lied about one part of his testimony at Simi Valley—that he had returned to the station house to report excessive force—wouldn't that cast doubts upon everything else he said under oath?

So if justice was the goal, the question about Briseno's testimony was reduced to whether Briseno lied or told the truth when he said he returned immediately to the Foothill Station to alert senior officers about an unreasonable beating.

You may recall that in order to accomplish such a mission, Briseno had only a couple of minutes to drive two miles on city streets, park his cruiser, enter the station house, go into the watch commander's office, and see on a computer system a message from Koon: "U just had a big-time use of force…. Big time." If that happened, Briseno told the truth. But it couldn't have happened.

The time frame alone is compelling evidence that he did not

return to the station house to file a report against his fellow officers. But that wasn't all of the evidence.

Stacey Koon also returned to the Foothill Station immediately after the incident. And there's visible evidence—the apartment guard's videotape of the scene after its conclusion—that Briseno's cruiser was still parked when Koon's black-and-white pulled away. Koon had to return immediately for a practical reason: He had to get a newly armed TASER to replace the one whose cartridges had been discharged on Rodney King. And multiple witnesses at the station reported seeing Koon immediately after the incident—the watch commander and his assistant, to name two. Significantly, no witness at the station reported ever seeing Briseno during that time. Had he rushed around as his story required, Briseno could hardly have gone unnoticed.

Briseno's attorney, Harland Braun, avers that his client did not lie at Simi Valley. Braun says the mere fact that Briseno was indicted along with Koon, Powell, and Wind suggests that the government agreed. "They [the prosecutorial team] never considered it perjury because they used it [the taped testimony]," Braun observes.

"If they believed Briseno was lying, why would they use his videotape? And if he wasn't lying, why did they indict him? They were using Briseno to try to cause problems with the defense, and one of my goals was to prevent them from taking advantage of that. And it worked, except that Judge Davies then allowed them to put that videotape in their rebuttal [near the end of the trial]. Why didn't they put it in their primary case?"

Kowalski agrees with Braun. Kind of. Kowalski acknowledged that the government knew that "some parts" of Briseno's Simi Valley testimony were not "accurate," but he and the prosecution team decided to "let the jury sort out" truth from falsehood. In a more formal motion, the prosecution argued that since the defense had not objected in the first trial to Briseno's tainted testimony, the defendants had in effect waived the right to subsequent objections based on perjury.

Sure Briseno didn't tell the truth, at least partially, at Simi Valley, the government conceded. But it was entitled to use those lies as "a false exculpatory statement" intended to "prove consciousness of guilt." In short, the government made a circular argument in an end run to get it both ways.

This kind of legal logic was put in clear perspective by Koon's attorney, Ira Salzman, in his closing argument. The government's use of the videotape, Salzman argued, was a "schizophrenic" presentation if he'd ever seen one.

"Briseno lies," Salzman told the jury. "He perjures. He's not giving truthful testimony. But everything [accusatory] he says about Sergeant Koon is correct. If the government really believed Mr. Briseno's testimony... why is Theodore Briseno sitting over there... as a defendant?

"The government had the gall, the utter gall to tell you that he's lying, and they put on lying testimony. Isn't that bothersome? Is that the truth? Is that right? What can one make of such a thing? When it helps the government's case, believe him [Briseno]. When it convicts Stacey Koon, believe him. When Ted Briseno testified in his own behalf, he's a liar. But if he says something bad about Stacey Koon, believe him. Don't believe him. Believe him. Don't believe him. Don't believe him. I'll just flip a coin and decide. That's not how justice is presented. That's not how cases are decided."

In the end, of course, the jury would demonstrate to Salzman that it is how some cases are decided.

Jury Conduct—and Misconduct

"[J]ust flip a coin and decide," Salzman said. In this case, a heads-or-tails verdict might have even been more fair than the one ultimately rendered.

How otherwise to explain the jury's decision to convict Koon and Powell and exonerate Wind and Briseno? If testimony that was at least partially tainted by acknowledged distortions was admitted, if important material that would have helped the defense was withheld, if witnesses were intimidated—if all of this happened, why were the two officers found guilty?

One reason may have had to do with trial strategies. Judge Davies was not a waffling, wavering Lance Ito. Davies came close to personifying the biblical image of a patriarchal jurist. He did not allow either the defense or the prosecution to argue endlessly over arcane points of law. Nor did he let witnesses ramble on or appear in a seemingly endless parade. He intended for the railroad to run strictly according to the law but also on schedule.

Accordingly, the defense put on far fewer witnesses at the federal criminal trial than at Simi Valley. Only Koon among the defendants testified (if you don't count Briseno's videotaped testimony). Expert witnesses were called only to make key points, and other direct defense or rebuttal witnesses summoned only if necessary to the core arguments. Salzman's aim, shared by his colleagues on the defense team, was to keep a good judge happy.

In contrast, the federal government simply produced more and better expert witnesses than the state had summoned at Simi Valley to counter a proved defense team of witnesses.

Of course, the prosecution had an edge here since the defense strategy was already known. This is one of the hazards in double jeopardy trials. Knowledge of what your opponent is going to do, when he's going to do it, how, and with whom gives a prosecutor an edge in constructing a successful strategy. As Kowalski said, "In the first trial they won the image battle; in the second trial, we won on image."

That's not altogether accurate, but the inaccuracy has nothing to do with the government's strategy. The fact is that the cops won at Simi Valley *despite* an image burned in the public's mind by the Holliday videotape. The defense won at Simi Valley by using facts to overcome a negative image.

This is not to criticize the government's success in image-building. To the contrary. Sergeant Mark Conta, for example, was a believable witness. He presented himself as an expert, and as a training officer at the police academy he had the credentials, if not the street experience, of Sergeant Duke, to back up his testimony. Moreover, at times Conta even appeared to be sympathetic to the indicted officers. His demeanor could reassure the jury that by accepting his testimony, the panel wasn't taking part in an LAPD campaign of vengeance against Koon, Powell, Wind, and Briseno. And, of course, as mentioned, Briseno's videotaped testimony, even if tainted, provided an opportunity to justify a guilty verdict against Powell for using too much force and against Koon for allowing it to happen.

In post-trial interviews with the media, members of the jury made two important points that reporters emphasized:

First, jurors said they were not influenced by what happened following the Simi Valley verdict—the riots and, for individual jurors in the state trial, the threatening phone calls, widespread accusations of racism, and other criticisms. Those had created such an emotional ordeal that some of the Simi Valley panelists were still undergoing psychiatric counseling a year later.

These statements by the federal court jurors raise questions. From the outside they appear suspiciously to mirror the government's contention that race was not a motivating issue in seeking the indictments—a transparent rejection of an obvious fact.[13]

Maybe the jurors were really not influenced by the mob of reporters that gathered daily in the sealed-off area outside the eighth-floor jury room where deliberations took place. Federal marshals had tried to cover the jury room windows to prevent anyone from looking out or in, but the covering was only frosting and didn't shelter the entire window. It was quite easy for jurors to stand on a chair and peer out at the media circus below, which they in fact did.

Maybe, too, the jurors were unaware of the Los Angeles riots sparked by the Simi Valley verdict. But if so, they were the only people in Los Angeles, probably the country, maybe even the planet, so blissfully ignorant, thanks to the Holliday videotape.

Harland Braun, Briseno's attorney, says it's silly to suggest that the jurors weren't influenced by the Simi Valley trial and subsequent violent anarchy. "This was a jury that *knew* that if they brought back a verdict of not guilty there would be another riot," Braun stated flatly in an interview.[14] He continued:

> Personally, I don't think there would have been another riot because I think the LAPD was prepared for the second trial.
>
> But that's not the point. The point is that the jury *thought* there would be another riot. The first [Simi Valley] jury was mocked by the public and in the media. People said they were a joke. People said they were idiots and bigots. And then a riot occurred. So who wants to be an idiot and a bigot and cause a riot?

Clearly they were influenced by that. Remember how close we were to a hung jury: The first vote on Koon was seven to five for acquittal. If we had gotten a hung jury I personally don't believe the government would have tried it again. I don't think they could have afforded to do that, because of the national repercussions. Remember, preparations were being made in every city in the country for a riot after this [federal] verdict.

But fears of more disorders weren't the only factor at work on the jury during the federal trial. Other influences were also being exerted on the jury to return a guilty verdict—influences not visible to the court, to the media, or perhaps even to some of the jury members themselves.

After the glare of publicity following the verdict had faded, at least three, perhaps four, members of the jury began having second thoughts about what they had done. By the spring of 1995, these jurors were willing to provide signed, witnessed affidavits about the reservations that had developed about the verdict.

The jurors will not be named here, because the affidavits almost certainly will be entered as evidence in the event another appeal of the verdict becomes necessary. If that occurs, the jurors' names will be made public. And if such an appeal is not forthcoming, then no useful purpose would be served by identifying them for the public opprobrium they almost certainly would receive from some groups for reneging on a guilty verdict they had earlier supported. Here's what they said in signed affidavits in early 1995:

> *Juror A:* My name is _____ and I was a juror on the federal trial of Sergeant Stacey Koon. I don't think Sergeant Koon should serve a day in jail. It's a waste of talent.... He was doing his job and I don't think Sergeant Koon was guilty of anything....
>
> I was upset when I heard about the original sentence [of thirty months] Koon received. Me and [three other jurors named] were not convinced of Koon's guilt and as I kept saying that I didn't see where he was guilty the other eight jurors reran the tape and said, "We can see it, why

can't you?" I felt some pressure not to create a hung jury because of the two months that we [had already] put in. The last part of the deliberations were on Koon and I got the feeling I was going to be held hostage until I swung over to a guilty verdict....

At the beginning of deliberations Maria[15] and [another juror] both said before we started looking at the evidence that "All of them are guilty—no ifs, ands, or buts."

Juror B: My name is _____ and I was a juror in the trial of Stacey Koon. I think the original sentence was too long and even more time would have been worse.... The windows [of the jury room] were frosted. I got a chair once and looked over the frosted windows. I was curious what floor we were on and I saw some cameras down on the street. Several jurors would compare their notes out loud with other jurors who had [also] taken notes.

Juror C: My name is _____ and I was juror number __ in the case of *U.S. v. Stacey Koon.*... There was one juror who seemed to have his mind made up before deliberations really started. One of the jurors came in right at the beginning of deliberations and what he said and the way he said it made me think he was biased from the start. I remember him telling a story about Sergeant Koon holding a TASER and King thinking it was a gun. We were discussing that during deliberations. I knew from my own recollections and from my notes that there was no evidence of that, and that the juror had just run with the evidence and made up a story that did not conform with the evidence. This juror also seemed to be in a real hurry to get a decision. He didn't want to give us a chance to go through our notes. We often discussed during deliberations, and back at the hotel, what we thought the judge was going to do. I remember [another juror] theorizing that the judge might call off the whole case because there might be adverse public reaction. This discussion happened while we were still deliberating....

There was frosted glass over the windows, but we were

still able to look out and see all the news media down below. We talked about that....

I thought that Maria at times had an agenda and wanted to follow that rather than participate fully in deliberations.

As endnote fifteen states, the "Maria" cited by two of the jurors was Maria Esquibel, a U.S. Postal Service worker in her late twenties. She is African American, one of two selected for the jury. But, as two of the jurors' statements suggest, she seemed one of the most influential members of the panel. Among other things, she led the other jurors in aerobics exercises during free time.

On the questionnaire the final seventy-five members of the jury pool had to complete, Maria Esquibel seemed to be perfect for both the defense and the prosecution. She provided a racial balance that would avoid the criticisms leveled at the Simi Valley jury, which had no black members. She said she had no preconceived notions about the case and had no personal experiences with the Los Angeles Police Department that might influence a decision one way or the other. She said she had an open mind about the case and could serve impartially.

What she didn't say—and wasn't asked—was that her father was a "one-time '60s radical who had ties with Black Panther Huey Newton and activist Angela Davis," as he was described by the *Orange County Register* in its highly flattering article (August 1, 1993) about her service on the jury.

Moreover, her father, Webster Moore, who in his youth "saw himself as part of a struggle against oppressive government," had been beaten by Los Angeles police officers during a student riot in 1971 and injured seriously enough to receive eighteen stitches, the article added. The newspaper story quoted Moore as saying that after the federal trial, his daughter was "really able to identify with another human being beaten by a power so great that he didn't have any recourse." Moore told the *Register* that he "had a special interest in the trial, and that it was a personal thrill seeing his daughter chosen as a juror.... 'I can only feel that I did something right [in raising her],'" the article quoted Moore as saying.

Another signed affidavit involved a fourth juror who boasted publicly about his prejudice against the cops and manipulating the jury to get a verdict. This panelist, *Juror D*, spoke to a college class in the Los Angeles area in May 1993, a little more than a month after the verdicts, about his service on the federal criminal jury. The professor of the class said in a signed deposition:

> In May of 1993 I spoke with *Juror D*. He told me he had been a juror in the case of *U.S. vs. Stacey Koon* and was interested in getting on various talk shows. He spoke of others who had gotten on talk shows. He told me about his interest in completing a movie deal to tell his story.... On May 20, 1993, *Juror D* came to talk to my two sections of Group Discussion. He spoke about his experience on the jury, and answered questions from the students.
>
> *Juror D* told my classes that he was a regular marijuana user, but he knew that marijuana users could not be jurors. He stated that before he was selected as a juror he was asked some questions on a lengthy questionnaire and by a panel of lawyers, but was never asked specifically if he is a regular marijuana user. He laughed as he recounted [how] their failure to ask him a specific question about his regular marijuana use allowed him to get on the jury....
>
> At one point *Juror D* was asked by one of the students how he felt about the defendants. *Juror D* angrily responded, "I hate those cops. They should be in cages." He then spoke about how "proud" he was that he had managed to convince seven jurors to vote for guilt.
>
> *Juror D* said that the jurors had stayed in the Hilton Hotel across from the University of Southern California. He said there was a security guard posted at one end of the hallway where the jurors were staying.... *Juror D* stated that he likes to drink. He talked about how proud he was that one evening he managed to sneak past the security guard, go down to the hotel bar, watch television, and read a newspaper.

After describing other minor escapades during deliberations— escapades that even though minor, were obvious misconduct—as related by the juror, the professor witness said:

> *Juror D* said that some of the jurors discussed how they
> were worried that there would be another riot if they voted
> to acquit the defendants....
>
> One of the students in my class... asked *Juror D* what
> he would do if the students called a television station and
> reported what *Juror D* had told them. *Juror D* said that he
> would deny having made any of the statements he made to
> the class.

So, in addition to governmental abuses of power to gain convictions, it would appear that some serious questions could be raised about whether the jury itself was fair and impartial, whether truth and justice were *its* aims.

Whatever the reasons, in the end the jury was able to justify its convictions of Koon and Powell almost entirely on the Holliday videotape, supported by Briseno's Simi Valley testimony and Sergeant Conta's explanations of use-of-force policies, explanations that were disingenuous even if not known to the jury.

And so, on April 16, after ten days of deliberations, the jurors concluded their work by finding Powell guilty of violating Rodney King's civil rights by using too much force to subdue King during a legal arrest and Sergeant Stacey Koon similarly guilty for allowing it to happen.

The next morning, on April 17, the verdicts were announced. Koon accepted the news with stoicism and no apparent physical reaction. Powell was visibly shaken by the verdict, his voice quivering slightly at one point when he responded to a question asked by Judge Davies. Koon and Powell left the courthouse and began preparing for the next steps in their continuing ordeal: consulting with attorneys on appellate procedures, accumulating records necessary to meet with officials from the U.S. Probation and Parole Office, and getting psychologically accustomed to the fact that they very probably faced prison terms.

Wind and Briseno, relieved at having survived two successive prosecutions, had yet to face more legal proceedings necessary to have the Los Angeles Police Department acknowledge some responsibility for the loss of wages and medical and legal expenses they had incurred since March 3, 1991. And all four officers still faced a civil trial in the suit Rodney King had brought against them.

The jurors were thanked by Judge Davies for their service and taken to Dodger Stadium on a bus for a final gathering before dispersing after more than a month and a half of sequestration. Like the O.J. Simpson trial jurors of later date, some members of the federal panel that had convicted the cops began contacting people they thought might be helpful in arranging talk-show interviews or selling book and movie rights.

Maria Esquibel was honored by having the story of her influence during jury deliberations included in a one-woman docudrama staged in Los Angeles. Entitled *Twilight: Los Angeles 1992*, it told about the tumultuous events that followed March 3, 1991—the Simi Valley trial, the riots, the federal prosecution, the ultimate conviction of Koon and Powell. The *Orange County Register* described Esquibel as having "the timbre of a Lauren Bacall" (even though she did not appear in the one-actress show), and the story reported that "critics raved" about the docudrama's portrayal of Esquibel's jury service. She had become, ever so briefly, a media starlet.

Now Judge John G. Davies would take center stage and the spotlight.

VI

A CONTROVERSIAL
SENTENCE

Why has government been instituted at all?
Because the passions of men will not conform to the
dictates of reason and justice, without constraint.

Alexander Hamilton
The Federalist, XV, 1787–88

A Victory for the Defense

U.S. District Judge John G. Davies was confronted with a difficult if not agonizing dilemma.

On the one hand, the court was faced with a jury verdict that wasn't
wholly consistent with the evidence presented. Yet it *was* the decision
the jury had made, and the jury had to be upheld. The question was
this: What kind of sentence could serve the elusive purposes of justice,
which had been distorted if not altogether perverted by the media and
uninformed public opinion based upon the media's presentation?

Unlike criminal penalties in most states, federal sentencing guidelines for someone convicted of a felony are set, rigid, and tough to bend. You commit a certain crime under certain circumstances, and you're assigned so many points. It's much like football, where each infraction has a prescribed penalty.

This is not to say that federal criminal penalties are wholly inflexible, but that a federal judge's rigidity or flexibility in imposing punishment is controlled by those guidelines. General court decisions in recent years have given federal judges some latitude in imposing penalties, but not much.

Consequently, with a guilty verdict rendered by the jury, the question facing Judge Davies was, what would be a fair penalty to impose upon Koon and Powell given the circumstances of the Rodney King arrest?

The evidence of guilt was mixed. Rodney King obviously was responsible for some parts of the incident; the officers, according to the jury, were responsible for other parts. The LAPD was not on trial for its official procedures, so it escaped judgment. The government wasn't on trial for the clear misconduct of its prosecutors, either. The only ones on trial were the two officers, who stood alone against the might and power and malice of the United States government. Only Judge Davies stood between that power to punish and the officers' vulnerability to the ruthless abuse of power. Only Judge Davies' fairness could protect Koon and Powell from harsh reprisals for offending the racial sensibilities of the media and the bureaucracy.

Judge Davies' office was flooded with letters arguing both sides: That the cops should be given the maximum allowable penalty for administering street justice to an offending black man, or that they should be given the minimum allowable by law or even probation because they were simply performing their duty with the tools they had been given.

One letter the courts find particularly useful in determining the severity of a penalty is the victim's impact statement. In such a statement the victim of an alleged crime describes the effect it has had on his or her life and usually asks the court to impose the maximum allowable sentence. Rodney King's victim impact statement fit that mold. But it also contained some comments that appeared to be paradoxical, at best, in light of both prior and subsequent events.

In the letter to Judge Davies, King (or, more precisely, his attorney at the time, Milton Grimes, since someone with less than a fourth-grade reading and writing comprehension could not possibly have composed such a letter[1]) wrote that his medical bills had totaled more than $189,000 and that the officers should repay him for those expenses, as well as pay a hefty fine, in addition to receiving a maximum prison term. This, King said, would "send a message to other police officers that the savage beating of unarmed citizens by those cloaked with the authority of law will no longer be tolerated."

OK so far. That's an understandable, even reasonable position for a victim to take. But then King (or Grimes) began to test the limits of truth, given King's history of encounters with the law.

His severe medical problems, King wrote, had caused "my wife... to devote numerous hours of her time to caring for me, care that normally would have been devoted to our children. My children, like my wife, feel the strain of this added burden." Never mind the prior (as well as future) accusations of spousal abuse or that under oath King said he didn't know the address of his children, who lived in the custody of his former wife.

The entire incident "has taken not only a physical toll but also a psychological toll," King wrote to Judge Davies, adding that his "prescribed medication alleviates some of the problems." He made no mention of probation reports on tests that showed use of such non-prescription medication as heroin and cocaine, which also have a profound impact on psychological stability.

"I find myself thrown into the depths of anxiety and despair by simple things like the sound of a siren," King wrote. These "depths of anxiety and despair" would be experienced by King in future months as the sound of sirens pulled him over to the roadside for charges of drunken driving and assault.

About the only thing King said in the letter to Judge Davies that had a ring of plausibility, considering the background of the entire affair, was a statement that he had become an unwilling symbol of minority complaints of police racism.

"By no choice of mine," King wrote to Judge Davies, "the March 3, 1991, beating has resulted in my becoming a symbol, emblematic of the history of police brutality against poor and minority people in America. I did not choose to be thrust into the public eye, and if

I had a choice, I would probably choose otherwise. However, for me there is no escape or turning back. With this new-found symbolism that has been thrust upon me as a result of the beating, comes awesome responsibility and much pressure. I find that I constantly worry about making the slightest mistake because the whole world will know of every indiscretion, and my family will be haunted thereby."

Well, of course King *did* choose his course. He could have submitted to arrest. But the statement is nonetheless revealing because it seemed that Rodney King finally had gotten the point: He realized that he was being used by minority politicians to advance their own interests.

In addition to the victim statement, two other sentencing recommendations—the government's and the defense's—were submitted. These will be dealt with momentarily, because one independent, unsolicited communication deserves mention. This letter could have been a model for the sentence Judge Davies ultimately rendered, although there is no evidence that it had such a direct impact. In addition, the government's reaction to it shows the lengths to which the Justice Department would go to guarantee that the cops do as much hard time as possible.

David A. Lombardero, a Los Angeles attorney and former chief counsel of the U.S. Sentencing Commission that wrote the federal guidelines in the mid-1980s, wrote Judge Davies pointing out the reasons a court could use to justify departing from established rules to give the cops a more lenient sentence than the guidelines ordinarily required.

Lombardero told Judge Davies in the letter that Rodney King's "wrongful conduct in evading, resisting and even taunting the police officers substantially provoked" the incident.

In addition, Lombardero noted that there was neither any allegation nor any evidence of a racially discriminatory motive on the part of the police officers in subduing Rodney King. This was important, because transgressions with racial motivation had been *the only* instances in which the government had pursued civil rights actions against cops until the Rodney King arrest. Lombardero told Judge Davies that in typical civil rights cases against police officers, motivation based on racial bias was "assumed" to be present.

Moreover, the former government lawyer said, "It is clear a substantial portion of the injuries sustained by Mr. King were properly inflicted in the performance of the officers' duty... [and] the [sentencing] guidelines obviously did not anticipate such a circumstance."

In summarizing his conclusions, Lombardero qualified his comments by stating that "I am not, and do not purport to be, fully familiar with the facts of this case, including the defendants' personal characteristics [that might influence sentencing]."

His comments must have struck a nerve, because the government quickly reacted. The Justice Department obtained a letter from the incumbent Sentencing Commission executive director saying, in effect, that Lombardero had been nothing more than a minor functionary of the commission, his title, "chief counsel," notwithstanding. Thus his comments shouldn't be taken seriously, the government suggested.

The most significant recommendations a federal court receives regarding sentencing come from the prosecution, the defense, and the U.S. Probation and Parole Office.

Of the three, the most independent obviously is the Probation and Parole recommendation, which conducts an objective review of all the facts. It looks at all of the materials submitted to the judge; interviews defendants and their lawyers, victims and prosecutors; and presumably arrives at an unbiased position. Ordinarily, all three recommendations—the defense, the prosecution, and the Parole Office's—are submitted directly to the judge in order to ensure neutrality.

But once again the government wanted to make sure that its pursuit of the officers couldn't be viewed as indulgent. The government wanted the harshest possible punishment. So prosecutor Steven Clymer submitted his recommendation directly to the Probation and Parole officer, Richard Griffis. That way Griffis wouldn't miss the implied message that the prosecution expected other government agencies to get on the team and play ball in punishing the officers.

Clymer's recommendation, which is to say the government's, asked that Koon and Powell be given unusually harsh penalties—seven to nine years for Powell, nine to ten years for Koon. To justify this vindictive severity, Clymer used some peculiar, albeit perfectly legal, logic. Among other points, he argued that the offenses for which Koon and Powell were convicted involved a felonious assault "with a dangerous weapon with intent to do bodily harm."

Well, that's certainly true, at least the part about the officers being armed, and no one ever disputed the point. But consider: Koon and Powell were policemen, bound both legally and morally to subdue a combative felony suspect who refused to obey legal commands.

Of course they were armed. Policemen on duty are always armed. Of course they intended to do bodily harm, once Rodney King resisted all of their efforts to subdue him peacefully. They intended to inflict as much pain upon King as needed, but only to gain his compliance with their orders. What should they have done? Taken off their guns, tossed their PR 24 batons away along with the TASER, and politely asked Rodney King please to allow himself to be hand-cuffed? Given Rodney King's behavior that night—from the eight-mile, high-speed chase to throwing four officers off his back, to absorbing fifty thousand volts twice from a stun gun, to either trying to escape or to attack Powell, and his constant attempt to rise while ignoring commands to prone out on the ground—such a scenario is the stuff of a *Saturday Night Live* satire.

Then Clymer argued that by testifying on his own behalf Koon had obstructed justice. Koon's testimony, Clymer said, represented "perjury... during the trial in this case when providing false justification for the beating of Rodney King." This could be proved, Clymer said, because "the jury's unanimous verdict necessarily encompassed a finding that defendant Koon had lied about the reasons for the continued beating of Rodney King."

This proposition is truly frightening in its implications, and not just because it comes from a prosecutor who encouraged Briseno's perjury in videotaped testimony from Simi Valley. Taken literally, it means that anyone who unsuccessfully offers a defense in a federal criminal trial should be punished for obstruction of justice, perhaps even perjury, if the jury doesn't buy the defense argument. That argument, if accepted by the courts, could lead to world-class double jeopardy. In the federal trial, the only demonstrable perjury or false testimony was provided by Clymer and the prosecution—Rodney King's waffling on whether the cops used the word "nigger" and his admission that he lied when it was beneficial, and Briseno's video-taped account at the Simi Valley trial about how he returned to the Foothill Station to report excessive force.

But Clymer's attempt to intimidate Parole Officer Griffis didn't work. When Griffis submitted his report to Judge Davies, he played it right down the middle. He outlined the options available to Judge Davies for imposing maximum or minimum penalties and the rationale behind either decision. It was Judge Davies's call.

It had taken the government precisely one year to accomplish its objective of getting somebody convicted and on the way to jail for the Rodney King episode. The federal indictments were handed up on August 4, 1992. Convictions of Koon and Powell were obtained on April 16, 1993. Sentencing was scheduled for August 4, 1993. The government gunslingers had taken only 365 days to put two more notches on their pistols.

But they were to be disappointed, sorely disappointed, with how Judge Davies viewed the entire matter. His sentencing memorandum reads more like a brief for the defense than an acknowledgment of the prosecution's success.

Noting that the government had "presented its case in great detail," that it would be "hard to imagine that the government overlooked any fact," Judge Davies said some factual matters remained unresolved. To impose a fair and just punishment, these matters must finally be put to rest. Therefore, he said, the court—meaning Judge Davies—would have to untangle the questions that remained unanswered.

Who was responsible for the episode?

First, Judge Davies said, King's "wrongful conduct contributed significantly to provoking the [officers]'s offense behavior."[2] Judge Davies wrote in his sentencing memorandum that trial testimony supported a finding that "Mr. King was engaged in illegal conduct *prior to and during* his arrest" (emphasis added). He continued:

> Mr. King was admittedly intoxicated while driving. Mr. King failed to stop his vehicle, even after he belatedly perceived the flashing police lights and sirens. Perhaps due to his intoxication, Mr. King was slow to comply with

police orders to exit his car. In any event, he failed to remain prone on the ground as the police ordered him to do.

Rather, Mr. King resisted Officers Briseno, Solano, Powell, and Wind. He attempted to escape from police custody. In doing so, Mr. King, a still unsearched felony suspect, ran in the direction of [Officer] Powell. He intended to escape into the unlit recreation area.

At this point, the officers' use of the baton commenced. The initial provocation for the subsequent course of events was Mr. King's wrongful conduct.

Indeed, the entire incident would have been avoided if King had merely obeyed basic traffic laws and pulled over when the California Highway Patrol officers first summoned him to stop by turning on their cruiser's flashing lights. "Had Mr. King pulled over… Koon, Powell, and the other LAPD officers would not have been summoned…. Koon and Powell did not seek out a victim; rather, their very presence at the scene was a consequence of Mr. King's wrongful conduct," Judge Davies wrote.

Did the officers have cause to fear Rodney King?

The cops' first analysis of King as dangerous was "reasonable," the judge continued. "This initial perception was reinforced when Mr. King rose from a prone position on the ground and attempted to escape, running toward Mr. Powell. Whether or not Mr. King actually presented a danger to either Powell or Koon, their perception of danger was reasonable. At this point on the [Holliday] video, the use of force begins, provoked substantially if not entirely by Mr. King."

Was the initial use of the batons to subdue King justified?

Based on the factors above, Judge Davies said that it was. So then, to explain the jury verdict:

When did that force become excessive?

Judge Davies wrote that after reviewing the videotape time and again, he believed that only the last nineteen seconds of the Holliday videotape could constitute an unlawful application of force. Everything that happened before was perfectly legal.[3]

Everyone in the courtroom could see where this was leading. It was headed toward a minimum sentence. Clymer, said the *Los Ange-*

les Times, "appeared stunned." Then Judge Davies explained that there were other factors that argued in favor of a "downward revision" of federal sentencing guidelines.

In addition to Rodney King's responsibility for provoking the incident, "defendants Koon and Powell have already sustained, and will continue to incur, punishment in addition to the sentence imposed by this court," Judge Davies wrote. Besides their vulnerability as former police officers to prison abuse, Koon and Powell "will be subjected to multiple adversarial proceedings [Rodney King's suit for civil damages] and stripped of their tenure by the LAPD."

Judge Davies continued ticking off the factors that argued in favor of a more lenient penalty.

"Third, while the offense of conviction involves a serious assault, there is no evidence, and the government does not argue, that Koon and Powell are dangerous or likely to commit crimes in the future."

And the fourth concerned the appearance of harsh punishment in violation of constitutional double jeopardy protection against vengeful prosecution. Judge Davies said, "Koon and Powell were indicted for their respective roles in beating Mr. King only after a state court jury acquitted them of charges based on the same underlying conduct. Under these circumstances, the successive state and federal prosecutions, though legal, raise a specter of unfairness."

Judge Davies made short work of the government's position that extra punishment should be imposed because they were armed when the incident occurred. "Police officers are always armed with 'dangerous weapons' and may legitimately employ those weapons to administer reasonable force," Judge Davies wrote. "Wherein an officer's initial use of force is provoked and lawful, the line between a legal arrest and an unlawful deprivation of civil rights... is relatively thin."

Similarly, Judge Davies didn't buy into Clymer's contention that the jury's finding of guilty meant that Koon's testimony on his own behalf represented perjury, wherefore Koon's punishment should be increased for obstructing justice.[4]

"Mr. Koon testified at the trial and denied having acted with the unlawful intent to refrain from protecting Mr. King from an unreasonable use of force. The government contends... that obstruction of justice applies here, reasoning that the jury's verdict against Koon necessarily constitutes a finding that Koon testified falsely. The court disagrees," Davies wrote.

"Although Mr. Koon's belief that he acted lawfully is a mistake, *as indicated by the jury's verdict*, the court finds that Koon's testimony reflects a personal belief... he held in earnest. Mr. Koon did not willfully intend to provide false testimony. That the jury chose to disbelieve Koon's testimony, or found it insufficient to prove lack of intent, doesn't establish that Koon committed perjury" (emphasis added).[5]

Given all of these factors, with the additional observation that "neither Koon nor Powell are violent, dangerous or likely to engage in future criminal conduct... [and] there is no reason to impose a sentence that reflects a need to protect the public from these defendants," Judge Davies issued his ruling: Koon and Powell were to serve thirty months each in a federal correctional camp, followed by two years' supervised release.

Federal sentencing guidelines do not specifically provide time off from a sentence for good behavior, but early release allowances can be accumulated by a well-behaved inmate at a rate of eighty days for each twelve months served. Accordingly, Koon's and Powell's sentences meant that each would be eligible for supervised release at the end of twenty-six months and possibly earlier if granted halfway house or furlough privileges ordinarily permitted to federal inmates who don't cause or get in trouble in prison.

As for restitution and fines, Judge Davies told Rodney King and the government to forget it.

King's request for $189,494.31 in medical bills, Judge Davies wrote, "is unsubstantiated and is best left for the pending civil action. Moreover, neither defendant is able, or is likely to become able, to pay restitution.... An order to pay restitution would place an undue burden on Mr. Koon's dependents. For these reasons, restitution will not be ordered."

The fines of $150,000 each for Powell and Koon sought by the government were out of the question, too, the judge wrote. "The pre-sentence report indicates that Koon's assets are essentially exhausted. He has five dependent children who will be unduly burdened if a fine is imposed. Powell is likewise unable to pay a fine, and unlikely to become able to pay. Accordingly all fines are waived, including the cost of imprisonment," Judge Davies concluded.

The Victims of Crime Act of 1984 requires the court to impose a special assessment of $50 on any defendant convicted on a federal felony charge. The assessment cannot be avoided or waived. Judge Davies ordered Koon and Powell each to pay the court $50. That was the extent of their financial penalty. The government got a financial return of $100 on its prosecutorial investment of more than $1 million. And the political return was even less, because civil rights and minority leaders remained sullen and unsatisfied.

The Empire Strikes Back

The defendants' attorneys were understandably pleased with the judge's analysis of the facts and assessment of penalties. Michael Stone, Powell's lawyer, told the *Los Angeles Times* that "the judge's findings were nothing short of a total vindication of the defense." Salzman expressed similar sentiments on Koon's behalf in a post-sentencing interview on the *McNeil-Lehrer News Hour* on public television.

Understandable, too, was the swift, sure, and predictable reaction from civil rights organizations, minority leaders, and a largely hostile media that all along had done so much to inflame public passions against the officers. And to drive home the point that these forces had an establishment constituency that listened closely to what they said, the LAPD went on tactical alert at 7:00 A.M. on the day the sentences were handed down, anticipating, perhaps, that the minority community would find anything less than maximum penalties unacceptable.

Within a week, members of the Congressional Black Caucus wrote Attorney General Reno urging her to appeal the sentence as too lenient. Shannon Reeves, director of the NAACP's Western Region, told the *Sacramento Bee* that "the judge appeared to put the victim on trial while accepting Koon and Powell as model citizens." The Reverend M. Andrew Robinson-Gaither, pastor at the Faith United Methodist Church in Los Angeles, said Judge Davies's "leniency indicates to us the system doesn't care about people of color." John Duff, president of the Los Angeles chapter of the NAACP, said, "This is a travesty of justice as opposed to a measure of justice." On NBC's *Today* show immediately after the sentences, Rodney King said he was "shocked" and "not satisfied" with the sentences.

U.S. Representative Maxine Waters, whose district embraces South-Central Los Angeles where the riots began, called the sentences a "kiss on the wrist." Paul Parker III, a relative of one of the defendants soon to stand trial in state court for beating white truck driver Reginald Denny during the 1992 disorders, told the *Los Angeles Times* that the sentences demonstrated that the riots were "justifiable." Parker said, "If there is no justice for blacks, there will be no peace."

Media reactions were equally severe. Columnist Dorothy Gilliam, writing in the *Washington Post,* said, "The logic [used by Judge Davies]… was stunning. In his lenient sentencing, he was an unreconstructed apologist for the police. In condoning the officers' behavior, the judge displayed strong racist overtones because he is, in effect, perpetuating a system already oppressive to people of color and the poor."

The *Phoenix Gazette* called the sentences "reprehensible," adding that "not only did he [Judge Davies] contradict the jury's message that police brutality is unacceptable, but he also handed the officers a moral exoneration." On August 7, the *Economist* of London, the highly respected British international magazine, called the sentences a "slap on the wrist," adding that "the people of Los Angeles were too emotionally drained to do more than utter a few grunts of disapproval" at the sentences.

To provide an idea of just how disappointed media critics of the officers were at the sentences, a page one story in the *Los Angeles Times* found consolation by speculating on what life in prison would be like for the officers. The story said soothingly that they would be "marked men," ranking "only a notch above child molesters" in the prison pecking order. Two weeks later, the *Los Angeles Times* even resurrected ancient history to support its belief that the sentences were too easy on the cops. The newspaper revived a year-old story that Powell had been reprimanded in 1992 for using excessive force in an incident that occurred in 1990.

This matter is worth brief examination, not because of media prejudice, but because it reveals to what extremes a vindictive LAPD management was willing to go to persecute Koon and Powell for embarrassing the department.

In May 1991, more than two months after the Rodney King episode, a use-of-force complaint was filed against Powell, Koon, and two other officers in connection with a domestic dispute that occurred on October 3, 1990. No plausible explanation for the delay exists, except perhaps the complainant's sniffing an opportunity to cash a ticket in the Rodney King publicity lottery, file a lawsuit, get booked on a talk show, appear in a story in a supermarket tabloid, and, hell, maybe even write a book.

Details of the incident are largely unimportant. Suffice it to say that the principal victim of the alleged use of force, someone who was not even the complainant, denied to investigators that he had been struck by Powell with a flashlight or that Koon had said "Fuck you" to one of the family members as the complainant had charged. The department quickly dropped the investigation of Koon and the other two officers. Powell, however, did receive a reprimand even though it could not be conclusively demonstrated that he had done any wrong. And this was because of an anti–street cop quirk in LAPD administrative procedures: When a complaint is proved against an officer, that officer can be punished administratively—suspended, even kicked off the force. When a complaint is disproved, as this one against Koon and the other two officers was, no action is taken. But if even partially sustained and neither proved nor disproved— as this one was, even though the alleged victim distanced himself from the complaint—the department can put a reprimand in an officer's file. And that is what happened to Powell in post–March 1991 as the LAPD scurried to distance itself from Koon, Powell, Wind, and Briseno.

Captain James McBride, Koon's Foothill Station boss on March 3, 1991 (and today a full commander on the LAPD), supervised the reopened investigation. He wrote a memo to the new chief on December 2, 1991, which said: "Unfortunately, in reviewing the summary and formal statements of the complainant and other civilian witnesses, the investigation in its present form does not provide sufficient information to support this allegation [of illegal use of force]."

The choice of words is troubling. Why was it "unfortunate" that the complaint could not be supported? Logic would suggest that the LAPD would be happy that the officers had been exonerated.

But it certainly was "unfortunate" for Powell that the charge against him could be neither proved nor disproved. Because on August 16, 1992, as Koon and Powell were preparing to stand trial on federal charges, Chief Williams wrote to Powell that his actions in the old incident represented "SERIOUS MISCONDUCT" and "if it were not for the expiration of the statute of limitations[6]... a *substantial* penalty would have been imposed upon you" (emphasis in original).

Then, to make sure that the LAPD had covered itself and that Powell (and presumably the media) hadn't missed the self-serving message, Williams wrote, in capital letters: "I AM THEREFORE IMPOSING THE MAXIMUM ALLOWABLE PENALTY AND HEREBY OFFICIALLY REPRIMANDING YOU."

To somebody facing prison time in the federal penal system, the penalty was laughable. But it was not pretty. It was still a case of kicking somebody who's already down. Powell was facing a federal trial. And one charge unresolved by the Simi Valley jury was still hanging over him.[7] You might even call Chief Williams's reprimand a case of excessive administrative force.

And now, with Judge Davies's sentence under a barrage of criticism from the media and minority leaders, the government was going to show Koon and Powell the real meaning of excessive force.

Koon and Powell sought to delay going to a federal work camp until the federal appellate process had been exhausted. It was a reasonable request and one with many precedents; almost every federally convicted felon who poses no threat to society is granted freedom while appeals work their way through the courts.

But in the cops' case it wasn't granted automatically. So they went into custody. But Judge Davies agreed that Koon and Powell represented no threat to fellow citizens and were unlikely candidates for fugitive status, and should therefore be permitted to remain out on bail. Koon and Powell were released and returned to their families.

The United States of America, as represented by Kowalski and Clymer, however, said no. These felons belong behind bars.

And so in the case of *U.S. v. Stacey Koon*, Kowalski and Clymer filed an emergency appeal with the Ninth U.S. Circuit Court of Appeals in San Francisco. They argued that bail should be denied under the Mandatory Sentencing Act, which was intended and is used primarily to keep drug dealers and violent criminals off the streets while the appellate machinery grinds forward. The government also asked that the thirty-month sentences be increased substantially.

In other words, the government wanted to impose post-sentencing punishments on Koon and Powell. Put it this way: Even if the officers were guilty of misconduct as the jury determined, it was for only nineteen seconds. In its appeal, the government wanted Koon and Powell to spend a minimum of almost four months in custody for every second of the offense.

Had that same standard been applied to Attorney General Reno, who assumed responsibility for the Waco disaster—the five-week standoff and ultimate deaths of more than eighty people—Reno would have been in prison until long after the starship *Enterprise* had returned safely to Earth.

Now the danger facing the two former police officers had gone beyond simple double jeopardy—dual prosecutions for a single act that occupied only nineteen seconds and whose legality was arguable. Now the officers faced yet another threat—and the threat was triple jeopardy.

VII

TRIPLE JEOPARDY

No man is to be brought into jeopardy more
than once for the same offense.

Sir William Blackstone
Blackstone's Commentaries on Law, c. 1775

Assault on the Fifth Amendment

The idea that a person accused of a crime should be tried once and only once for the same offense is almost as old as human history. Since the pre-Christian era, most legal systems—and certainly those in Western societies—have honored this concept.

This protection was contained in the Justinian Code, which stated in 529 A.D. that "the governor should not permit the same person to be again accused of a crime of which he has been acquitted." And the Justinian Code itself was based on earlier writing by Roman legal experts. Later, the protection against double jeopardy was a visible thread in the fabric of medieval England's common law.

In America, protection against double jeopardy was guaranteed by the Massachusetts Body of Liberties in 1641, the first bill of rights in what would become the United States of America 140 years later. The protection also was guaranteed by several other prerevolutionary

American colonies when they adopted bills of rights based on the Massachusetts model.

The framers of the federal Constitution considered protection against a vengeful and powerful government—or government leaders—so important that that protection was included in the first ten amendments that embody the American Bill of Rights. The Fifth Amendment to the Constitution says:

> No person shall be held to answer for a capital, or otherwise infamous crime, unless on a presentment or indictment of a Grand Jury, except in cases arising in the land or naval forces, or in the militia, when in actual service in time of war or public danger, *nor shall any person be subject for the same offense to be twice put in jeopardy of life or limb;* nor shall [any person] be compelled in any criminal case to be a witness against himself, nor be deprived of life, liberty, or property, without due process of law, nor shall private property be taken for public use without just compensation [emphasis added].

The language is simple and direct: A person cannot be tried twice for the same offense.

Thus as the Supreme Court said in 1874, "If there is anything settled in the jurisprudence of England and America, it is that no man can be twice lawfully punished for the same offense."

But in the twentieth century, the U.S. Supreme Court began taking a more activist role in interpreting the Constitution, and by the 1950s a series of decisions had rendered the double jeopardy guarantee almost meaningless. The biggest breach torn in the Bill of Rights' Fifth Amendment guarantee against multiple prosecutions came as a result of what's known as the "dual sovereignty" doctrine. It's an outgrowth of the theory that the interests of federalism are separate and apart from the interests of the state, that each draws its political powers from a separate source—that is, different constituencies—even if those sources are the same people. Put another way, "dual sovereignty" supposes in theory that the federal and state governments are separate and equal. In practice, however, today it means that the federal government is more equal than the states.

What "dual sovereignty" means to double jeopardy is, basically, that a single alleged offense may violate laws in more than one political jurisdiction. When this happens, each "sovereign," or government, has the legal authority to prosecute the defendant.

Throughout most of the nation's history, the dual sovereignty doctrine wasn't too troubling in criminal cases, because there was little overlap in criminal offenses between the federal government and the states. For the most part, federal crimes were confined to a narrow range of rare national or international offenses—piracy, smuggling, treason, counterfeiting, and the like—while the states concentrated on a broader range of more common crimes of a localized nature—murder, robbery, theft, assault, and so on.

But the overlap between federal and state criminal offenses became broader with the growth of federalism, a concept stressed forcefully by Supreme Court Associate Justice Felix Frankfurter. From the 1930s through the 1960s, Frankfurter's views usually prevailed in the double jeopardy cases that came before the court. Today, as a general rule, under case law involving dual sovereignty a defendant's double jeopardy protection is violated only under one or both of two circumstances: First, if the federal and state governments cooperate and act as a team although the prosecutions are separate, and, second, if the separate charges leveled against a defendant in separate cases are essentially the same.[1]

A landmark dual sovereignty case involved a man named Bartkus who held up a savings and loan in Illinois in 1953. Bartkus was first tried by the federal government for robbing a federally insured bank. He was acquitted by a federal jury.

The state of Illinois then tried Bartkus for robbery, a state crime. Bartkus was convicted and sentenced to life in prison. Bartkus appealed to the Supreme Court, arguing that his Fifth Amendment right to protection from dual prosecutions had been violated since he had already been exonerated in a federal trial. In 1958, the Supreme Court upheld the state sentence because, the Court said, the state's interests were different from the federal government's. Therefore, the double jeopardy clause did not apply, the Court said. The majority opinion was written by Associate Justice Frankfurter.

The decision brought a stinging dissent from Associate Justice Hugo Black, a strict believer in the literal language of the Constitution and Frankfurter's persistent rival for intellectual leadership of the Court for three decades. The "precisely defined" boundaries of the Constitution and the Bill of Rights were manifestly violated in the Bartkus case, Black said. His *Bartkus* dissent continued:

> The court apparently takes the position that the second trial for the same act is somehow less offensive if conducted by the federal government and the other by a state. Looked at from the standpoint of the individual who is being prosecuted, this notion is too subtle for me to grasp. If double punishment is what is feared, it hurts no less for two "Sovereigns" to inflict it than for one. If danger to the innocent is emphasized, that danger is surely no less when the power of the state and federal government is brought to bear on one man in two trials, than when one of these "Sovereigns" proceeds alone. In each case, inescapably, a man is forced to face danger twice for the same conduct.

Now, Bartkus may have been guilty and no doubt was for the state court to impose such a severe penalty—life imprisonment—for a single act of robbery. But the question at hand is this: After one jurisdiction lost the case—through either sloppy prosecution or the defendant's proved innocence—was it appropriate under the Fifth Amendment to try him again?

And if the state had lost the second trial, what then? Could Bartkus have been tried a third time or yet a fourth time on still more charges by either jurisdiction? Could the state have indicted him for using a weapon in the commission of a felony? Could the federal government have made a case for violating national firearms laws? How long could prosecutions go on? Until the government-desired conviction was obtained?

This was the demon that tormented Justice Black. The double jeopardy clause ranked at the top of the list of guarantees of individual liberty, right along with freedoms of speech, religion, and assembly, Black believed. In 1957, before his *Bartkus* dissent, Justice Black wrote in another double jeopardy case:[2]

The underlying idea, one that is deeply ingrained in at least the Anglo-American system of jurisprudence, is that the state with all its resources and power should not be allowed to make repeated attempts to convict an individual for an alleged offense, thereby subjecting him to embarrassment, expense, and ordeal and compelling him to live in a continuing state of anxiety and insecurity, as well as enhancing the possibility that even though innocent he may be found guilty.

This statement could have been tailor-made for the federal government's prosecution of Koon, Powell, Wind, and Briseno following their acquittal in Simi Valley. There's no question that the officers have been subjected to "embarrassment, expense, and ordeal and... a continuing state of anxiety," not to mention that Koon and Powell's guilt of a federal crime is arguable since they were found innocent by the state on almost identical charges.

A curious but relevant sidelight in the dual sovereignty theory is that it applies only to venue relationships between the federal government and the states and not between the United States and foreign governments. If a defendant has been tried in a foreign court and acquitted for an offense that also violates U.S. federal laws (drug dealing or money laundering, for example), the U.S. government will not prosecute the accused a second time—under the Fifth Amendment guarantee. The question obviously follows: If the Justice Department respects judgments of foreign courts, why doesn't it grant the same respect to state courts? If the Justice Department is willing to trust the legal systems of such rogue nations as Cuba, Iran, or Iraq, why wouldn't it trust California? More to the point, did the federal government so distrust the reliability and judgment of the California court system that it felt compelled to enter the case only after the state jury had failed to convict Koon, Powell, Wind, and Briseno? Did the Justice Department do so because the state prosecution was sloppy or corrupt, or did the federal government enter the case simply because the state lost at Simi Valley?

All available evidence suggests the latter. The state was serious about prosecuting the officers. No one ever accused the Los Angeles District Attorney's office of insincere motives in prosecuting the case. The state didn't drag its feet and certainly didn't go easy on the officers during the trial. So it must be assumed that the federal government acted only because the state didn't win and for no other reason.

The next question then is, why did the state take the lead in prosecuting Koon, Powell, Wind, and Briseno? If the federal government was so serious about the matter, why didn't it take the first shot? One possible, even probable, reason is that the California constitution specifically rejects the dual sovereignty doctrine. If you've been tried once by another jurisdiction and either convicted or acquitted for an alleged offense that violates California laws, too, you can't be tried again in California. Period. End of story.

Which means, of course, that if the federal government had proceeded first against Koon and his officers and they had been found innocent, as they were in the state trial at Simi Valley, the government would never have gotten another chance to carve out its pounds of flesh. And the state would have had no opportunity to prosecute. The officers would have walked. Minority politicians and civil rights leaders and their media sycophants would have had no opening to demand that the officers be afflicted with another prosecution.

Which brings us to another exception to Fifth Amendment protection against multiple prosecutions, an exception that began to take on added importance in the 1960s when the civil rights movement acquired momentum in the South.

On numerous occasions in the South of the sixties, private citizens and law enforcement officers had been charged under state statutes with acts of violence against civil rights activists. On at least four widely publicized occasions, these acts involved murder. But all too frequently, all-white local juries would find their "good ol' boy" neighbors innocent of any wrongdoing, despite incontestable evidence to the contrary. A case that leaps to mind involved the twenty-one Klansmen, including a sheriff, a deputy sheriff, and a municipal cop, who were accused of murdering Chaney, Schwerner, and Goodman. *Life* magazine memorialized these thugs in a picture showing the accused law enforcement officers and their Klan accomplices in a federal courtroom, laughing and chewing tobacco as they awaited arraignment on federal charges for a crime the state wouldn't prosecute. Such was the conspiracy of silent bigotry the

Justice Department and the civil rights movement faced in the South in the 1960s.

That picture galvanized the rest of the nation and many people of goodwill in the South. Among other results, the public outrage it generated prompted the Justice Department to accelerate its war on racism. So in the mid-1960s government lawyers dusted off statutes and a constitutional amendment from the post–Civil War era guaranteeing all Americans equal protection under the law. Using these handy tools, the government stepped in and successfully prosecuted a number of civil rights cases that state prosecutors either wouldn't touch or tried to lose, among these the Mississippi Klansmen who violated Chaney's, Schwerner's, and Goodman's civil rights by murdering them.

Thus was another vent cut in the fabric of the Fifth Amendment. It was a departure motivated for all the right reasons and employed at the right time in history. But it proved to be so flexible that it came to be applied in ways unimaginable to the framers of the Bill of Rights.

Race and Double Jeopardy

To understand fully how the Justice Department cynically manipulated the precedents of dual sovereignty and the Southern experience of the 1960s, it is necessary to return to the Simi Valley trial and the state prosecution.

The reason for moving the state trial to Simi Valley in Ventura County from Los Angeles County, which had been ruled out because of prejudicial publicity, was this: Because of crowded dockets and geographical necessity, the choices were limited to Simi Valley in nearby Ventura County; Oakland, in the San Francisco Bay area; and Orange County, which is south of Los Angeles. Oakland was the state's best bet because it was overwhelmingly black and liberal. But Oakland was out of the question; it was so distant that it would have imposed an almost impossible travel burden on both the prosecution and defense. Orange County, a conservative bastion, would have been best for the defense. Simi Valley was a logical compromise because it was the most favorable geographically, not because it was best for the cops.

Unlike the South in the sixties, no evidence even suggested that the Simi Valley jury acquitted the four officers because the jurors were bigots. Everyone just assumed it was so. The absence of African Americans on the jury was interpreted as prima facie proof that racism played a role in the trial. And, in fact, race did enter into the Simi Valley proceedings, but not in the way you might think.

Ventura County, where the state prosecution was moved because of pretrial publicity, has a much smaller African American population than Los Angeles County, where the episode occurred. But it is not true that no blacks were potential jurors in the state trial. Indeed, the court went to great pains to guarantee that the pool of potential jurors from which the panel would be drawn reflected the racial makeup of the venue. Ventura County is about 5 percent black; representation of African Americans on the jury pool for the Simi Valley trial was slightly higher than the general population of Ventura County.

Why, then, were there no black jurors?

Quite simply, because a local member of the NAACP made personal contact with most if not all of the potential black jurors. It remains unclear whether the NAACP activist tried to influence any potential juror's opinion in the case. Certainly no one was ever accused of jury tampering. But the contact was sufficient to taint all but one of the black jurors, in the presiding judge's opinion, and all but this one were removed from the pool over the prosecution's objections. The lone remaining black in the jury pool was rejected by the defense for reasons that had nothing to do with race.

Yet the myth that race played a role at Simi Valley persists. And this myth, when viewed in the context of the O.J. Simpson murder trial, reveals in stark clarity the uncompromising hypocrisy of minority and civil rights leaders and liberal critics of the Simi Valley trial.

Minority activists argued that there could not be a fair trial in Simi Valley because of the small black population. This position assumes that the phrase "jury of peers" means peers of the alleged victim—Rodney King. But the U.S. system of jurisprudence is of course predicated on the assumption that it is defendants, not victims, who should be judged by their peers; victims aren't judged, period. Moreover, "peer," as defined by *Webster's Dictionary*, is someone "of equal standing" under the law. Minority leaders' use of the term further assumes that a peer is defined by race and not simply by citizenship, and this twists the interpretation of "jury of peers" to the breaking point.

But let's assume for a moment that the minority critics' position is absolutely correct, that victims rather than defendants are entitled to peer judgment in a criminal trial, and that the judicial definition of "peer" requires giving weight and consideration to race.

In the O.J. Simpson case, the victims, Nicole Brown and Ron Goodman, lived in the predominantly white and wealthy Brentwood neighborhood of Santa Monica and were murdered there. Using the exact standard minority leaders applied in the Rodney King episode, the jury in the O.J. Simpson case should have been drawn from a mostly white and wealthy pool of potential jurors who live in the Santa Monica neighborhood or someplace very much like it. This didn't happen, of course; the Los Angeles district attorney took pains to pacify minority leaders by ensuring that the trial was held in downtown Los Angeles, where the population and jury pool is heavily weighted with blacks and Hispanics.

You can see the contradiction coming like a freight train down the track. Under the race-based logic advanced by minority advocates, to criticize the makeup of the Simi Valley jury for allegedly excluding poor blacks is to criticize the O.J. Simpson jury for *excluding anyone who was not white and wealthy.* And don't ignore the corollary, which is this: If O.J. Simpson got a fair jury and a fair verdict, then the jury composition and verdict at Simi Valley were equally fair for Stacey Koon, Laurence Powell, Timothy Wind, and Theodore Briseno. And race prejudice struck another ugly note. Because of racial pressure, the Fifth Amendment protection against double jeopardy didn't stand a chance. The dual sovereignty weakness and the historical background of civil rights prosecutions in the South in the sixties saw to that.

In short, the federal prosecution in the Rodney King episode reeked of racial politics, so much so that even a significant number of federal and state judges believed the second trial violated the officers' constitutional protection against multiple prosecutions. A poll taken by the American Bar Association in July 1993 reported that 21 percent of 401 state and federal judges surveyed believed

Koon and Powell were convicted unconstitutionally in the federal trial.

Granted the poll was heavily weighted with state judges who might be more likely to resent the federal government's intrusion into state judicial proceedings—30 percent of them said the police officers' rights were violated. Still, a sizable minority of the federal judges—fully 10 percent of those surveyed—agreed. They thought the officers were wrongfully charged by the federal government to begin with and that the injustice was compounded by trial and conviction.

Divisions over the double jeopardy issue were sharpest in the larger legal community. The breach wasn't between defense lawyers and prosecutors, as one might assume. It was between civil rights lawyers and attorneys with more traditional views on the Constitution.

Morris Dees, a nationally recognized civil rights advocate with the Southern Poverty Law Center in Alabama, told the *American Bar Association Journal* that the dual sovereignty exception "does not offend my sensibilities of fair play."[3] In the Rodney King episode especially, Dees said, "the state charges of excessive force probably didn't fit nearly as well as the federal charges. There clearly was a violation of Mr. King's civil rights…. If it is so egregious a violation of one's civil rights, federal prosecutors should just move ahead."[4]

Dees' position is disingenuous at best, and deliberate, self-serving liberal distortion at worst. Surely the state charges—using excessive force under color of authority—and the federal charges—violating Rodney King's civil rights by using excessive force and failing to protect him while in official custody—are not wholly or even substantially different offenses. Furthermore, one of the charges—the one against Koon, for failing to protect Rodney King's civil rights while in official custody—was demonstrably false; even the edited Holliday videotape clearly showed that *Rodney King was never in custody* until the very end of the incident when he voluntarily submitted to arrest, when he held up his hands and said, "Please stop."[5]

In any event, both charges stemmed from the same incident, and evidence presented at both the state and federal trials was essentially the same—in fact, almost identical. This is what bothered other lawyers, such as Pasadena attorney William Harris, who was quoted in the same article. "A criminal defendant who passes through the crucible once and survives is entitled to some peace,"

Harris told the *American Bar Association Journal.* "The danger [of the dual sovereignty exception] is that it tends to be invoked only in response to politically unpopular or politically incorrect attitudes."

And therein the rub: The federal trial of the officers was a politically motivated prosecution if ever one existed. Some people tried to inch their way around the political factor but it was slow and painful going.

Take Laurie L. Levenson, for example, a professor of law and evidence at Loyola Law School in Los Angeles. You've probably seen her commenting on television on the trials of O.J. Simpson, the Menendez brothers, and other high-profile criminal cases. Among her professional colleagues she's known as a "talking head" lawyer— an attorney who glories in media exposure and is unlikely to espouse a position the media might find inconsistent with their views. She conceded to the *American Bar Association Journal* in the same (August 1993) article that the second federal trial generated "political interest," but insisted that it was not a political trial. "President Bush didn't indict the four officers; the grand jury did."

Well, yes. Technically. But grand juries are controlled by U.S. attorneys. U.S. attorneys are controlled by the Justice Department. The Justice Department is controlled by the White House. As noted in chapters V and VI, the grand jury process is acutely sensitive to political influences not visible to an untrained eye. The reading on the political sensitivity thermometer rises even higher when the White House is involved. And you can't get much more White House involvement than a president going on national television to order that the cops be expeditiously prosecuted.

A more balanced view was aired in the *American Bar Association Journal* by Professor Sheldon Nahmod of the Chicago-Kent College of Law. Nahmod said that in addition to the Holliday videotape and change of venue in the state trial, the federal prosecution was set apart by the "political factor… that impugned the integrity of the entire criminal justice process." By itself, Professor Nahmod suggested, the political pressure alone might have been enough to impel the government to drill a second hole when the first one turned up dry.

When you cut through the legal rhetoric, what you got down to was this: Civil rights activists believed the second trial was appropriate and legal, primarily because race and cops were involved. Supporters of the cops believed the federal prosecution was politically motivated and unconstitutional under the double jeopardy clause. More neutral observers had reservations about the constitutionality of the proceedings, but understood the political pressures behind them.

Nowhere was the division over double jeopardy more painful than in the American Civil Liberties Union (ACLU), which historically has opposed the doctrine of dual sovereignty on the grounds that it is a sly legal charade used by prosecutors to get around the Fifth Amendment.

A few months after the Los Angeles riots, after the officers had been formally charged but not yet indicted, the national ACLU board, at the behest of the Los Angeles chapter, voted to suspend its traditional opposition to the dual sovereignty exception. Six months later, the national board had second thoughts and voted by a narrow margin to resume its policy of opposing multiple prosecutions under the dual sovereignty argument. The national board's vote prompted the Los Angeles chapter to reject the parent organization's position and go on record as supporting the dual sovereignty exception—but only in cases where cops are accused of violating someone's civil rights.

Ramona Ripston, executive director of the ACLU of Southern California, said in an article co-authored by Paul Hoffman, legal counsel for the local organization, that "what is at issue is whether this prosecution [of the four officers] is faithful to the bedrock tenets of the Constitution."[6]

Then, in a dialectic leap over the barriers of reason and the language of the Fifth Amendment, Ripston and Hoffman qualified the "bedrock tenets of the Constitution." The "heart of our position," they wrote, "is the sense that the federal government should be able to bring federal civil-rights prosecutions after state court acquittals, at least in some cases, to ensure that abuses of power by those acting under the color of law are addressed under relevant federal civil-rights laws."

In other words, according to Ripston and Hoffman, sometimes it's OK to plead double jeopardy protection, other times it's not. If ever a classic example of situational ethics existed, this is it.

What Ripston and Hoffman didn't say was perhaps more important than what they did say. As former U.S. Sentencing Commission Counsel Lombardero observed in his letter to Judge Davies, race is "assumed" to be a factor in all prosecutions of law enforcement officers for civil rights violations if the cops are one color and the victim another.

But race was never mentioned by Ripston and Hoffman. You see, civil rights activists have their own coded language, just as bigots have their trigger phrases that mean more than they actually say. When Ripston and Hoffman wrote that *"in some cases"* the federal government should have the power to use the dual sovereignty exception to hurdle the double jeopardy obstacle erected by the Fifth Amendment, what they were really saying was that this authority should be exercised in cases involving accusations of racist-inspired conduct.

All this notwithstanding, neither the ACLU of Southern California nor anybody else was ever able to sustain an accusation that race was a motive in the Rodney King episode. Neither could it argue that the state didn't aggressively prosecute the officers in Simi Valley the first time out. Nor could a good legal argument be made that the racial makeup of the Simi Valley jury was a deliberate attempt to edge around justice, particularly since the jury pool was tainted by the meddling of an overzealous member of the NAACP.

After the Simi Valley verdict, the ACLU of Southern California objected on two counts:

First, the state shouldn't have allowed a change of venue at all, because the officers could have gotten an impartial jury in Los Angeles. But this argument wouldn't wash, since a *Los Angeles Times* poll before the state trial reported that 86 percent of LA residents surveyed had seen the Holliday videotape and 92 percent of them believed the cops had used their batons too freely.

Second, the Southern California ACLU contended that the dual sovereignty exception permits the federal government to prosecute in civil rights cases. But this position directly contradicted the national organization's long-standing opposition to suspending the Fifth Amendment.

In short, there was no reason at all to trash one of the Constitution's fundamental guarantees of liberty—except racial politics.

Legal Maneuvering

The opposite side of the coin is that for much the same reason—the dual sovereignty exception—double jeopardy was not the sturdiest legal peg Koon could hang an appeal on to reverse both the conviction and the government's prevention of bail during the appellate process. Even so, it had to be put into play.

One reason was that it seemed the most obvious ground. The question of double jeopardy was what most puzzled nonlawyer observers. The answer to that question, as stated above, was dual sovereignty, which had been upheld repeatedly during the twentieth century by the Supreme Court.

But appellate lawyers also knew that almost every double jeopardy argument rejected by the Supreme Court was won by a single vote. Thus there was hope that a less activist court would reverse the doctrine. This hope was encouraged by a shift in the Supreme Court back toward the center of constitutional philosophy beginning in late 1994.

At that time, the Supreme Court began to retreat from the activist posture it had assumed since Earl Warren was named chief justice by President Eisenhower. One reason for this shift was the addition of two new swing justices, one of them Stephen Breyer, formerly chief judge of the First U.S. Circuit Court of Appeals and a prominent member of the commission that wrote the federal sentencing guidelines. Another factor was the heightened visibility and participation of conservative Associate Justice Clarence Thomas, a Bush appointee. In 1995, for example, among other decisions, the Court diluted the long-established use of federal police powers under the interstate commerce clause of the Constitution, and followed this up by weakening civil rights laws mandating affirmative action programs.

The double jeopardy pleading could not be ignored, because it was pure law and not based on legal technicalities. As such, it represented the base foundation of constitutional law that occupies the Supreme Court's deliberations. A less activist Supreme Court might be willing to review double jeopardy exceptions in a different light.

Several other grounds for appeal were less clear-cut and hence more compelling from the standpoint of legal precedent than a double jeopardy pleading. Some of these:

- Use of the videotape of Briseno's Simi Valley testimony violated another's defendant's rights because Briseno had been exposed to Koon's statements during the LAPD's Internal Affairs administrative investigation.[7] Since Koon's statements had been compelled—he could have been summarily fired for not cooperating.

- Sergeant Conta's testimony similarly was tainted, because during the state trial he had heard statements by a prosecution witness who had been exposed to compelled statements by Koon and Powell.

- Government prosecutors had made inflammatory comments in closing arguments, violating a rule that prohibits prosecutors from using language "calculated to arouse the passions and prejudices of the jury"—passions and prejudices that, as shown earlier, needed little calculation to be inflamed.

Koon's lawyers had asked the Ninth U.S. Circuit Court of Appeals to hear the case *en banc,* which means they wanted the entire appellate panel to decide the case. Koon's lawyers' reasoned that every judge has a hot button—a judicially sensitive nerve that might prompt a vote to reverse.

Given all of the arguments being presented on Koon's behalf, the more judges, the more chances that the defense might score points on appeal. And the Ninth U.S. Circuit Court of Appeals has twenty-eight judges.

But the effort failed. The Ninth Circuit voted to have the appeal heard only by a three-judge panel. And the panel, headed by Senior U.S. District Judge James M. Fitzgerald of Alaska, rejected virtually every argument Koon's lawyers presented.

Double jeopardy was a done deal, the court said, a matter sufficiently decided by legal precedent under the dual sovereignty exception. No evidence existed to indicate that the federal trial was a "sham," or that the federal government was a "tool" of state authorities. And it was OK for federal prosecutors to use evidence collected by the state. And so the gavel crashed down on the double jeopardy clause of the Fifth Amendment.

Similarly, the Briseno videotape was acceptable to use, the panel of three judges decided. The videotape had been sufficiently laundered of any information that Briseno hadn't witnessed himself, so Briseno hadn't offered any opinions tainted by compelled testimony—and never mind that Briseno had perjured himself in testimony at the state trial.

Likewise, the three judges ruled that Conta's testimony had not been poisoned by hearing testimony at Simi Valley. The witnesses whose testimony Conta heard had not talked about any details of Koon and Powell's statements, newspaper accounts of Koon's testimony notwithstanding, so Conta couldn't have known what Koon had said, the judges ruled. Soviet jurists at the height of Stalin's purge of opponents would have admired such logic.

As for misconduct by government prosecutors, Judge Fitzgerald and his colleagues largely dismissed arguments by Koon's lawyers that prosecution arguments were intended to "inflame" the jury.

That may have been because the jury needed no more inflammation, given the packs of reporters and TV personnel everywhere outside the courtroom and Maria Esquibel inside the jury room. Still, Kowalski and Clymer got their knuckles gently rapped for saying that the Holliday videotape evoked "horror and outrage" from "Paris to Tokyo." This wasn't a fair criticism of the prosecution, since the defense had used the same phrase during Rodney King's testimony. Even so, the panel of judges said the comments "went beyond the bounds of appropriate advocacy and were improper." Therefore, the jury's ability to be impartial in deciding guilt or innocence was "not materially affected" by the prosecutor's remarks.[8]

Then the three-judge panel moved on to Judge Davies's downward revisions of sentencing guidelines. And it systematically ground each one into a fine legal powder.

Losing jobs and other additional penalties suffered by the officers, Judge Fitzgerald wrote, didn't justify a reduced sentence because the justice system "cannot and does not attempt to be the sole arbiter of the consequences of criminal acts."[9] That Koon and Powell were former police officers and vulnerable to abuse wasn't important, the court ruled, because almost anybody could make that argument—even drug-dealing gang members. That Koon and Powell posed no likely threat to society wasn't sufficient reason for easier sentences, either, Judge Fitzgerald's panel ruled, because they already qualified for the most trustworthy grouping assigned to convicted defendants and "a departure below that [higher sentencing level]… cannot be appropriate."

Successive prosecutions by the state and federal government? Double jeopardy? That matter had already been decided, the appellate court ruled. As far as Rodney King provoking the beating and the officers being armed, the circuit court specifically rejected Judge Davies's reasoning; rather, the sentencing guidelines suggested a more severe than lenient penalty because the cops were armed agents of the government entrusted with official authority and Rodney King was an unarmed civilian.

And so it went. Just as Judge Davies ticked off reasons why Koon and Powell should get minimal penalties, Judge Fitzgerald listed reasons backing the government's request for more severe punishment. "We therefore vacate the sentences [given by Judge Davies] and remand for resentencing consistent with this [appellate court] decision," Judge Fitzgerald concluded.

It was a discouraging defeat for Koon and Powell, but it did not destroy all hope. The entire twenty-eight member panel voted on whether to hear the appeal "en banc," and although the circuit court does not release results of the balloting, it quickly surfaced that at least a third of the panel didn't agree with the decision not to let the entire court hear the argument—indicating a strong bloc of support on the appellate court for the officers' position.

One judge removed himself from the case for unstated reasons, leaving twenty-seven eligible to vote and fourteen the required majority. It is not known how many voted to reject the *en banc* request, but nine of the circuit judges dissented from the opinion.

More significantly, the dissent was written by Judge Stephen Reinhardt of Los Angeles. Not only was Judge Reinhardt regarded as perhaps the most liberal judge on the Ninth Circuit bench, but he was a former member of the Los Angeles City Council and Los Angeles Police Commission and thus thoroughly conversant with law enforcement matters generally and the LAPD in particular.

In addition to these credentials, which hardly suggest an indulgent attitude toward the officers, Judge Reinhardt is the husband of Ramona Ripston, of the ACLU of Southern California, who argued so ardently for the dual sovereignty exception to the double jeopardy guarantee.

The Reinhardt dissent was yet another indication of how deeply divided the Los Angeles community had become over the Rodney King episode. One can only speculate on how spirited evening conversation must have been at the Reinhardt-Ripston dinner table in the months following the federal trial, conviction, and sentencing.

The first issue Judge Reinhardt addressed in his dissent was whether the officers should be permitted freedom on bail as appeals and counterappeals inched through the judicial pipeline.

On September 12, 1993, as Koon and Powell prepared to go into custody, Judge Reinhardt landed squarely on the officers' side. "Because the court refuses to take this case *en banc*," Judge Reinhardt wrote, "we are forcing Stacey Koon and Laurence Powell to go to prison pending their appeal, even though nobody suggests there is *any* risk that they will flee or that they will present *any* danger to the community" (emphasis in the original). The alternative, he said, would be to "have subjected them to unjustified incarceration without any reason at all."

Put another way, by denying bail the officers would be exposed to triple jeopardy.

The federal law requiring detention during appeals except in special circumstances simply didn't apply to Koon and Powell, Judge Reinhardt reasoned. Congress, he wrote, obviously "did not intend to require detention for *everyone* convicted of a crime of violence" (emphasis in the original).

This legislative purpose was demonstrated by the principal sponsor of the 1991 Mandatory Detention Act, Senator Paul Simon of Illinois. Judge Reinhardt quoted Senator Simon as saying during debate on the measure that "this legislation would ensure that dangerous individuals be kept where they belong... and prevents [them] from re-entering the community where they pose a danger and can commit further offenses." But no one had ever suggested that Koon and Powell were dangerous. "They are no longer on the police force, so they are no longer in a position to harm anyone else in the community the way they harmed Rodney King," Judge Reinhardt wrote. "Nor is there any reason to believe that they would pose a danger to the community in any other respect."

Most important of all was the hardship and injustice that would be worked upon Koon and Powell if their appeals ultimately proved successful, Judge Reinhardt said. "We force Koon and Powell to commence serving a prison term that may be overturned on appeal. We do so despite the fact that there is no rational reason why they should be [kept in custody] while this case is decided." Then he concluded: "If they would not present a danger to society over the next several months (and I am aware of no evidence that they would), and if they would not flee (and no one suggests that they will), there is simply no justification for denying them bail."

These preliminary comments about the decision to deny bail by his colleagues on the Ninth Circuit Court were harsh enough. But Judge Reinhardt saved his big guns for a dissent filed in January 1995, after Koon and Powell had been in the federal correctional system for more than a year. In this dissent, he moved beyond the bail issue to the circuit court's decision to send the original sentences back to Judge Davies for more severe penalties.

"The sentences ordered by Judge Davies were severe indeed," Judge Reinhardt wrote. "Neither law nor justice requires that they be set aside or that any longer prison term be imposed." Only by "stretching truth to reach its result" and casting aside "the basic principles that should underlie judicial sentencing, even in the age of the [federal] guidelines," could the three judges who made the decision justify their action. "It is only by exalting the rigid calculations of charts and tables over the judgment of human beings that the panel reaches its conclusion that Judge Davies was too lenient" with Koon and Powell, Judge Reinhardt wrote.

In addition, Judge Reinhardt chided the majority for the court's secret vote to deny Koon and Powell a full hearing, a vote that did not tally with the opposing sides' lineups except for the three judges who signed the majority opinion and the nine who dissented. "Information... is necessary in order for the public, the legal community, and the academic world to assess the *en banc* process itself," Judge Reinhardt said.

Then, in a provocative aside hinting that something more than judicial fair play was involved in the decision, Judge Reinhardt wrote that "it would surely be of interest to those who study the courts if a series of *en banc* calls failed even though supported by a majority of the judges who actually voted." This suggested that the nine dissenting judges may have actually been a majority of the justices who cast ballots, but Koon and Powell's request failed because it hadn't been approved by fourteen of the twenty-seven eligible judges.

"In any event," Judge Reinhardt wrote, "the public has a right to know how each judge who has life tenure has performed all aspects of his judicial functions. Public scrutiny and accountability are the only checks there are on us, other than impeachment." Few citizens would disagree.

Finally, Judge Reinhardt put his colleagues on notice that sending the case back to Judge Davies for resentencing was likely to be reversed on appeal by the Supreme Court. Pointedly, Judge Reinhardt reminded the Ninth Circuit that the flexible interpretation of the sentencing guidelines used by Judge Davies had precedent in an opinion written by no one other than Associate Supreme Court Justice Stephen Breyer when he was on the First U.S. Circuit Court of Appeals. And the rejection of Koon and Powell's appeal, Judge Reinhardt said, "squarely conflicts" with Justice Bryer's written opinions.

Still and all, the Reinhardt dissent didn't address the issues of guilt or innocence; it criticized the legal process after sentencing. And Koon's position from the very beginning was that his conduct and that of his officers on March 3, 1991, had been wholly appropriate under the circumstances. From first to last, Koon sought nothing but the vindication that had been endorsed by the Simi Valley jury, a vindication subverted by a blatant legal and publicity play on racial politics.

Even so, the Reinhardt dissent was enough to lift Koon's spirits in February 1995 as he moved from Camp Parks in California to the detention compound overlooking Sheridan, Oregon, in the scenic Willamette River Valley. Although he had lost in the Ninth U.S. Circuit Court of Appeals, the Reinhardt opinion—a dissent that came from the least likely end of the political spectrum—provided hope that the system eventually would produce an impartial, evenhanded, equitable judicial decision free of political passions. His case was headed for the Supreme Court.

Winning a First Round

Technically, Koon and Powell's appeal was a request for a *writ of certiorari* (pronounced sir-she-oh-rah´-ree) from the Supreme Court. The Latin phrase means "to be informed." In legal terms, the writ is a command issued by a superior court to lower courts to provide the higher court with a particular case record so that it can be thoroughly reviewed for irregularities or errors that might have been committed at any time during the investigative, indictment, trial, sentencing, or appellate process.

In Koon's appeal, the writ was asking the nation's highest court to review virtually the entire case to determine if justice had been served as required by the Constitution. More specifically, the appeal asked the Supreme Court to pay particular attention to the double jeopardy issue, denial of bail, and the Ninth Circuit's demand that a more severe penalty be imposed.

At this final level of judicial consideration, the facts of the incident of March 3, 1991, were not an issue. The Supreme Court deals with law, which is not always related to facts. It receives thousands of appeals for rehearing each year and is able to consider only a handful. Most *writs of certiorari* are turned away without comment. In order to get the Court's attention, a plea for reconsideration must be approved by two of three judges who are assigned to read the appeal. Which means, of course, that an appeal must involve grave constitutional issues and be powerfully persuasive if it is to gain the attention of the full court.

Koon's appeal to the Supreme Court was filed in April 1995, after he had already been imprisoned for eighteen months. Two months later, in June 1995, the government filed its response by asking the Supreme Court to reject the request to review the case. By this time both sides were like two experienced boxers who had fought many times before. Both the government and Koon's lawyers knew what the other side would say well before they said it.

Koon's appeal would not be too different from his appeal to the Ninth Circuit, although some new arguments would be injected on constitutional grounds. The appeal would include double jeopardy, contradictory opinions about sentencing guidelines at the appellate court level, and conflicts between Rodney King's constitutional rights and those granted equally to Stacey Koon.

The substance of the government's response was just as predictable. The dual sovereignty exception overrode the double jeopardy plea, Judge Davies's lenient penalties violated federal sentencing guidelines, the Mandatory Sentencing Act justified denial of bail during the appellate process, and no trial errors violated Koon's constitutional rights.

On September 27, 1995, the Supreme Court announced it would hear Koon's appeal. It was a victory that beat the odds, which were heavily weighted against him. Koon's attorneys had successfully challenged the might and power of the Justice Department and the White House—at least in the first round.

But it was only a partial victory. The Court refused to reconsider questions of possible trial errors that might reverse the jury's guilty verdict—such questions as whether using Briseno's videotaped testimony from Simi Valley violated Koon's constitutional right to confront an accuser or whether the testimony of other government witnesses was tainted by exposure to Koon's statements made during the LAPD Internal Affairs administrative investigation. Rejected, too, was the double jeopardy issue.[10]

Nor was the victory final. The full Court might decide after hearing oral arguments and a full review that the government's position was right. Should this occur, the case will go back to Judge Davies. Then Koon and Powell will face genuine triple jeopardy.

If the case is returned for a new sentence, Koon and Powell will face the grim prospect of returning to prison for as much as six and a half to seven and a half years, which was what the government requested. That's the worst that could happen.

But Judge Davies might exercise one of several other options available to ease the impact of renewed punishment. He might decide that the officers have already been sufficiently penalized, free them, and wait to see if the government will continue playing hardball and pursue the matter. But given Judge Davies's reputation as a play-by-the-rules magistrate, that is unlikely. Equally unlikely, for the same reason, is for Judge Davies to neglect to put the order onto his docket, as other federal district judges have done in resentencing cases they've had returned on appeal, thus delaying the matter indefinitely.

The best bet is that Judge Davies will find some compromise ground; for example, an increase in the duration of post-confinement supervised release from the two years he originally ordered.

Whatever the result, Koon has vastly improved his chances for the vindication he has sought from the outset. Simply by agreeing to hear the appeal, the Supreme Court has cast doubt on the legitimacy of the federal government's prosecution of the Foothill Four—a prosecution that has reeked of vengeful injustice from the very beginning.

Moreover, even though the Supreme Court refused to rehear the case for a reversal of the guilty verdict, it is almost certain that Koon and Powell will appeal for a new trial. New facts have emerged since the federal jury found them guilty, facts that could provide a basis for arguing that the trial in Judge Davies's court was poisoned by improprieties. Primary among these are evidence of the government's illegally withholding Brady material, especially regarding Sergeant Conta's testimony regarding whether the "swarm" was an officially sanctioned LAPD procedure on March 3, 1991, when that sanction didn't come into force until after the trial was over and the officers in prison; the government's use of Briseno's testimony, at least a part of which was demonstrably false and thus contaminated everything he said; and, finally, suggestions of inappropriate behavior or outright misconduct by some members of the jury.

If finally vindicated, Koon almost certainly will seek enormous damages from the city of Los Angeles for the ordeal he has endured. Powell, Briseno, and Wind doubtless will do the same. The evidence is clear that some of the city's elected officials and some individuals in the police department joined in a loose and probably unplanned but nonetheless effective conspiracy of silence to ensure that all judicial proceedings arising from the Rodney King episode were pointed at the four officers, rather than the policymakers who were actually responsible for the way the incident played out. The ultimate monetary cost to Los Angeles could make the $3.8 million awarded to Rodney King look like pocket change.

So the story of the Rodney King episode isn't over. It is likely to go on for years. And in the meantime, the lives of millions of people have taken a different turn in the road because Rodney King drank too much beer one night and failed to stop when he got caught speeding.

VIII

WORLDS TURNED
UPSIDE DOWN

The order is rapidly fadin'
And the first one now will later be last
For the times they are a-changin'.

Bob Dylan
"The Times They Are A-Changin,'" 1963

Sweeping fires of social change often are ignited by a single, accidental spark.

In a very real and literal sense, Rodney King's failure to stop in the early morning hours of March 3, 1991, when a California Highway Patrol cruiser's red and blue lights first flashed in his rearview mirror, kindled fires and wrought changes in everyday life.

Because of the Rodney King episode, minority leaders believed their criticism of racist cops had been validated. Because of the Rodney King episode, Los Angeles burned. Because of the Rodney King episode, guilt and innocence are determined not by facts but

173

by racial politics. Because of the Rodney King episode, the entire concept of criminal justice in the United States has lost its moorings.

The Rodney King episode has affected every inhabitant of the United States. It has resulted in worse, not better, law enforcement—a proposition that can be demonstrated statistically and anecdotally. This certainly is true in the nation's inner cities, where violent crime—especially black-on-black crime—is most prevalent.

You see, the American people are inconsistent. On the one hand, they demand safe streets. On the other, they are horrified, as they were by the Holliday videotape, to see what safe streets sometimes require. Politicians such as Presidents Bush and Clinton, Attorney General Reno, former Los Angeles Mayor Tom Bradley, and former LAPD Chief Daryl Gates promise citizens that their streets will be made and kept safe. Yet they ignore the bitter realities of street-level police work and then callously turn their backs on and punish the frontline troops who have to do the dirty work in the trenches. Politics is politics, not public service.

What happened on March 3, 1991, was not an isolated, aberrant event. At this juncture, critics will say, "Aha!—you're right—racist cops are everywhere."

The prevalence of police racism is arguable, but whether it is or is not, it doesn't apply here because race had nothing to do with the arrest of Rodney King. Maybe Rodney King and his lawyers said it did, but not even the government was foolish or dishonest enough to make that assertion. If racism existed in the Rodney King episode, it was nourished by minority politicians, civil rights leaders, and an ideological media, all of whom assumed race was involved because Rodney King is black and the cops are white.

But the incident was not an aberration because something very much like the Rodney King episode occurs almost every day somewhere in the United States, and these occurrences have nothing to do with skin color, either. They are prompted by violent, resisting suspects who will not submit to being placed in custody. Indeed, they vilify cops, they try to steal cops' guns and shoot them with the cops' own weapons, they barricade themselves in a house with a hostage and an arsenal of weapons and dare cops to try and enter—as Stacey Koon's would-be assassin did on Thanksgiving Day 1995.

Sometimes a cop has to use force to subdue a violent suspect. Just read your local newspaper, perhaps look at some of your neighbors, and you'll be forced to concede this is true.

Remember Edward Nowicki, the former Chicago cop who testified for the defense at the federal trial? *"If you'd taken an isolated incident from my career and shown it out of context like the Rodney King arrest, it could have looked worse than the King incident. "*Ask any veteran street cop if the Rodney King arrest was a one-time, isolated event, and you'll get a cynical laugh.

Or at least you would have before the Justice Department launched its campaign to put the cops who arrested Rodney King behind bars. Today, these same street cops are in retreat. When a cop is confronted with a violent suspect, the Rodney King episode leaps to mind. The cop threatened by a combative suspect thinks first not about how the situation can be handled best, with a minimum use of force and least exposure to injury for both suspect and cop. Instead, his or her thoughts are on departmental punishment, loss of job, loss of pension, maybe even prison time like Koon's and Powell's, if the use of force is second-guessed. Consequently, and obviously, streets are less safe today than they were before March 3, 1991—especially in America's inner-city combat zones.

This retreat is not confined to Los Angeles. Listen to John Driscoll, retired assistant chief of the Dallas Police Department. Driscoll was known by his department's frontline officers as a street-cop manager, a law enforcement executive who would stand solidly behind his troops. He still maintains close relationships with many of the officers he once commanded, and this is what he's hearing:

> It's taken away the middle ground. No officer's afraid to arrest somebody—when you get right down to it, nobody's afraid to shoot somebody if they have to. But it [the Rodney King episode] has narrowed the gray area where an officer used to feel he or she had the discretion to use force as needed. That's gone.
>
> In the past an officer wouldn't hesitate to take any action necessary to bring an incident to a close. Now, though, they feel that any discretionary act is looked upon as a maximum use of force. In turn, a lot of action simply is

not taken, action that in the past would and should have been taken.[1]

Not only has the impact of the Rodney King episode made officers less bold, it has made life more dangerous for citizens who rely on police protection. "The safety of officers, of citizens," Driscoll says, "is jeopardized by overly cautious action—a timid use of force, if you will—against the suspect. And so today sometimes the officer just looks away, rather than taking an action and being judged for weeks and months to come. The bottom line is that this [attitude] puts more officers in jeopardy, it puts more citizens in jeopardy."

Echoes from the Rodney King episode reverberated in squad rooms throughout the nation. From Seattle, Sergeant Howard Monta wrote, "There will be no way to measure how many officers may lose their lives or become seriously injured... from being hesitant to act in their own defense, or defending themselves less aggressively because of fear of persecution or prosecution for doing their job."[2]

But nowhere has the impact been more palpable than on the Los Angeles Police Department. Cliff Ruff is a twenty-year–plus veteran of the LAPD and president of the seven thousand–member Los Angeles Police Protective League, the union for officers up to the rank of lieutenant. Ruff says the entire affair has "had a dulling effect on police work everywhere, but especially in Los Angeles." The federal government's prosecution after the officers had been acquitted in Simi Valley "sent a clear message that whatever you do is going to be subject to Monday-morning quarterbacking.... It's on every officer's mind," Ruff says.[3]

Senior managers of the Los Angeles Police Department also sent a message when they turned their backs on Koon, Powell, Wind, and Briseno. David Zeigler, chairman of the board of directors of the Police Protective League, said in a pre-sentencing letter to Judge Davies that the organization had received an increasing number of complaints about low morale because of a "lack of support" after the Rodney King arrest. "It is bad enough that the officers regularly face the consequences of this," Zeigler continued, "[but] these consequences pale in comparison with the prospect of serving time in federal prison under the... dimensions of double jeopardy imposed on police officers by the federal government."

If the Rodney King episode closed the coffin on LAPD morale, the O.J. Simpson affair nailed it shut. Not only was the LAPD accused of sloppy police work while investigating the Simpson case, the department also had to suffer the consequences of seeing Detective Mark Fuhrman plead Fifth Amendment protection against self-incrimination when questioned about whether he had perjured himself when he testified that he had not used racial slurs to describe minorities in the ten years prior to the trial or, worse, whether he had planted and distorted evidence to prove guilt of minority suspects. For minorities, the Fuhrman tapes provided audio evidence of police racism in the King case—no matter how unalike the two cases were.

And the media, of course, also linked the Fuhrman incident with the Rodney King episode. A signed *New York Times* editorial page column on September 11, 1995, by Brent Staples said, "First came the LAPD's savage videotaped beating of Rodney King. Now comes what black Americans are calling the 'soundtrack' for the King beating, the racist ramblings of Mark Fuhrman." The headline read: *"The Rodney King Soundtrack/*Mark Fuhrman's America, Los Angeles Style."

To connect Mark Fuhrman's racist comments with the racially neutral arrest of Rodney King by Sergeant Stacey Koon—an officer who once gave mouth-to-mouth resuscitation to a black male prostitute infected with the AIDS virus—is hypocrisy of such outrageous proportions as to defy decency and rational thought. It can only be assumed that writer Staples didn't know what the hell he was talking about.

The link between Fuhrman and the Foothill Four was even made by the LAPD management, and this hit the street cops hard. However dishonest the link, the two incidents, taken together, almost wholly demoralized the department, said Los Angeles Police Protective League President Cliff Ruff.

In a trade publication article about the incidents, Ruff said, "The message we have been getting from the City Council, the Chief [of police], the Police Commission and the *Los Angeles Times* about how to do our jobs is don't do anything. Don't use force. Don't shoot. Just smile. Wave. Do the dog-and-pony show."[4]

Given all of this, it's not surprising that there's been a slowdown in law enforcement in Los Angeles, and it harms all citizens.

Statistics show that Los Angeles police officers aren't being as responsible today as they were before March 3, 1991. Take, for example, a category called "officer-initiated calls." This occurs when an officer sees a possibly criminal act in progress and, doing his or her job as required, voluntarily goes out on a limb to report it. It's the sort of thing cops are supposed to do.

Well, the LAPD computers say that in the four years following the Rodney King incident "officer-initiated calls" declined by a startling 41 percent. Why? The explanation is obvious: Either the good citizens of Los Angeles are committing fewer crimes, a wild supposition at best, or the cops are turning a blind eye to judgment calls that might prompt an Internal Affairs investigation or, worse, prosecution by the state or, worse yet, by the federal government.

And there's more. As retired Assistant Chief Driscoll of the Dallas Police Department observed, officers aren't being as aggressive as they once were. That may satisfy some minority critics, but it also means citizens, and officers, of all races are in more peril.

According to data provided by the LAPD, total uses of force between 1990 (the year before the Rodney King incident) and 1994 dropped by 31 percent, from 3,406 to 2,347. And, significantly, uses of force involving the PR 24 baton plummeted by 90 percent, from 501 in 1990 to 41 in 1994. Los Angeles street cops have gotten the message—use your baton and you're liable to go to jail.

Another result has been that some cops can't get away from the Los Angeles Police Department quickly enough. Voluntary resignations rose from 1.3 percent of the LAPD's total strength in 1990 to 1.8 percent, by more than a third, in just the first ten months of 1994.

Charlie Ford is an example.[5] Ford worked as a street cop on the LAPD for five and a half years before resigning in late 1994 to take a job in Vancouver, Washington. During the 1992 riots, a looter grabbed Ford and dragged him across a rocky, glass-strewn parking lot. He was injured, and his uniform shredded. He sought in vain for reimbursement for the uniform—the department wouldn't pay, and it cost Ford $150 of his own money to replace gear that had been damaged while on duty. After the riots, Ford was attacked and ambushed five times. In one of the incidents, he was shot at by a seventeen-year-old girl firing a .45-caliber pistol, whose slug can rip a teacup-size hole as it exits a human body. During these ambushes, Ford's greatest fear was not getting killed but whether his department would charge him with excessive force if he returned fire.[6] That's when he knew he had to resign from the LAPD. His wife, Nancy, told *American Police Beat,* "This job has been hell since Rodney King."

If the fallout from the King episode on our police forces chipped away at our collective and personal safety, the blow to our legal system has been near disastrous. The presumed guilty tag tied around the necks of the cops from the start by the media and civil rights community, and the second trial's verdict condemning two of them to prison because of their color—white—led smoothly and inexorably to the verdict in the O.J. Simpson trial.

The black community—or at least black leaders—saw the Simpson murder trial as one more black-versus-white confrontation and nothing less. O.J. Simpson, a black millionaire who for years was fully integrated into and feted by the white community, suddenly became a black victim railroaded into standing trial for the brutal murder of his white ex-wife, Nicole, and an apparently chance visitor, Ron Goldman. Bloodstains, gloves, DNA evidence, a past history of extraordinary spousal abuse—none of this mattered. O.J. Simpson is black. That was enough.

This time it was easy. The word went out, as it had before: Unless the jury behaved appropriately—which is to say racially correct—riots could erupt, just as they had before. The jury bowed obediently, just as it had before. The verdict came in: Not guilty. O.J. Simpson walked out of the courtroom a hero. Justice had once again been held hostage to racial politics.

After the Foothill Four's second trial, blacks paraded the scalps of two white men, while the black felon who caused the episode counted his millions of dollars in damages earned through criminal behavior. In the O.J. Simpson affair, two white people lay dead in their own gore; the black man tried for their murder was found innocent, acclaimed by blacks, and returned to the golf courses.

The message is clear: We, the people of the United States, have been condemned by our own government to a system of justice that can aptly be called trial by race. If the question of right and wrong involves a black person and a white person, justice has become quite simple: If black you're innocent, if white you're guilty.

The lives of thousands of people, perhaps hundreds of thousands of people, have been touched by this new concept of justice. The families of Nicole Brown Simpson and Ron Goldman have been devastated, living with what they perceive as brutal injustice.

People intimately involved in the Rodney King episode are no different. Begin with Stacey Koon and Rodney King.

Koon's future is unclear because of legal uncertainties, but he continues steadfastly to believe that his actions were wholly within the law and that he was sacrificed as a pawn to political ends. Substantial evidence, outlined in this book, exists to support this belief—that the government of the United States, along with the Los Angeles political establishment, LAPD management, and an enthusiastic media, deliberately and willfully ignored, suppressed, or distorted evidence proving that Koon and his officers acted within the limits of the law in the early morning hours of March 3, 1991. But whatever happens, character suggests Koon will survive.

Rodney King's future is more clouded. He remains secluded, protected by people whose motives may not be altogether in King's best interests, although that is something only King can decide. King's attorney, Steven Lerman, says his client is busy giving speeches at elementary schools, urging kids to get an education, and taking kids on fishing trips as his own father had done.[7] The image might be true, but it hardly reconciles with the public record of arrests, drug use, and other incidents that have comprised King's rap sheet since March 3, 1991.

Other stories circulated by King's admirers include fanciful tales that he intends to buy a farm and perhaps write poetry. Perhaps these also are true, but there's still the knotty matter of the encounters with the law King has had since the federal trial that remain unresolved at this writing.

One important question is, what happened to the money King won in his lawsuit against the city? In May 1995, a Los Angeles television station, reporting on King, who had just avoided arrest in a domestic-violence incident involving King's wife and his brother, quoted King as saying that he had only about $500,000 left of the $3.8 million settlement from the city of Los Angeles. King's legal

fees could easily have absorbed a considerable amount of the settlement. In addition, King's former wife reportedly won a child-sup-
port settlement for an undisclosed amount. So King, this time, can
be taken at his word: He now has less than 15 percent of the $3.8
million he won from the city.

Then there's **Laurence Powell**. Like Koon, Powell was released
from custody to enter a halfway house, in his case in September
1995. And his future is in many respects tied to Koon's. If Koon wins
on appeal, Powell will probably also win. If that occurs, Powell will
have the same options open to Koon of appealing the original federal trial and verdict and then, if successful, suing the city of Los
Angeles for back pay, retirement benefits, workers' compensation,
and enormous damages for a variety of reasons.

Again like Koon, Powell genuinely believes he committed no
illegal acts on March 3, 1991. Powell has written that he believes he
was physically threatened by Rodney King, a belief sustained by that
portion of the Holliday videotape that was edited out by the media.

But unlike Koon, Powell's time in federal custody may have been
more difficult emotionally because his idealism doesn't seem to have
been tempered as much by the more realistic, and somewhat cynical, view Koon has developed about the influence of racial politics
on the entire episode. In an interview, Powell said he always believed
cops were the good guys and the justice system works for good guys.
"When you're singled out, though, you start to see things differently,"
he added.

Yet Powell's time in federal custody wasn't altogether grim. While
in the federal work camp at Boron, Powell became engaged to be
married. And he has developed an outside support group, largely
through the efforts of his mother and father, retired Lieutenant Ed
Powell of the Los Angeles Sheriff's Department. To raise money for
their son's defense, the Powells have sold copper bracelets like those
that memorialized U.S. prisoners of war during the Vietnam con-
flict and T-shirts that bear a sardonic slogan mocking the LAPD's
proud pledge that the role of a Los Angeles police officer is "To
Protect and To Serve." Powell's T-shirts say: "To Protect and To
Serve—Time."

Powell says he doesn't know how he'll earn a living in the future.
As long as his conviction stands, he cannot be a law enforcement

officer. And although he went to college and studied physics he did not graduate; the job market holds few opportunities for non-degreed physicists. "I don't know what I'll do," Powell said. But whatever it is, he added, "It certainly won't be in Los Angeles."[8]

Timothy Wind, the probationary officer riding with Powell the night of March 3, 1991, has experienced extreme difficulties. Wind was first fired by former LAPD Chief Daryl Gates. Then, after Wind was found innocent at Simi Valley, Gates promised to reinstate him. But the promise was canceled by former Philadelphia Police Chief Willie Williams when Williams replaced Gates as chief of the Los Angeles Police Department.

In the summer of 1995, Wind was earning $9 an hour working with the Culver City, California, Police Department. But despite his having been found innocent in three consecutive trials, civil rights leaders pressured the Culver City Police Department to fire Wind. The department refused to dismiss Wind without cause, but he was given an auxiliary job ordinarily assigned to high school kids or Explorer Scouts interested in police work as a career. Before joining the LAPD, Wind had been a veteran police officer in Kansas with eight years of service.

Wind's wife was pregnant when she testified at the civil trial and she suffered a miscarriage shortly afterward. Wind himself experienced such extreme stress that he developed severe intestinal disorders and had to undergo surgery. By the summer of 1995 he owed more than $35,000 in personal debts. His marriage was dissolving, and his future extremely uncertain. In the summer of 1995, he was thirty-five years old.

Theodore Briseno is a police outcast not so much because he testified against his former colleagues, but because he offered demonstrably false testimony that got those colleagues convicted while Theodore Briseno walked. He is now working as a private security guard in Los Angeles and is "psychologically disabled," according to his attorney, Harland Braun. "The blacks think of him [Briseno] as one of the four white cops, and the cops think of him as a Benedict Arnold of some kind. He wants to go back on the police force, but whether he's psychologically able to do so is another thing." In any event, the question of returning to the LAPD is probably out of the question; the department refused to rehire

Briseno although, like Wind, he was found not guilty in three different trials. Briseno has suits pending against the city of Los Angeles
for workers' compensation claims and loss of pay.

As for **Harland Braun**, he remains a celebrated criminal attorney in Los Angeles and often appeared as an expert television com-
mentator during the O.J. Simpson trial.

Braun says he wishes he had been Stacey Koon's lawyer in the
federal trial: "I think it was a winnable case from the defense point
of view, with a slightly different defense strategy," Braun said in an
interview.[9] "The defense should have been, 'People, after looking
at the video we screwed up, we didn't intentionally hurt anyone, so
it wasn't a civil rights violation.'

"But other than that, Koon took the tack that we did the right
thing and we'd do it again…. You end up giving the jury no way out
other than saying these guys either did the right thing or the wrong
thing. They had no case on Stacey until he got on the stand and
took full responsibility. Knowing Stacey, though, he couldn't have
done anything else. And he's telling the truth as he sees it."

Koon's attorney, **Ira Salzman**, says his views on how the law is
administered have been forever altered by the experience.
Salzman is not a courtroom novice; he was an assistant district
attorney in Los Angeles for five years after graduating from South-
western Law School and since 1988 has been in private criminal
defense practice.

"It wasn't until I became a defense lawyer, particularly representing Stacey Koon, that I acquired a deep understanding of the Bill of
Rights," Salzman said in an interview.[10] "It's not something intellectual with me [now]. It's in my heart, it's in my gut. I always thought
I was a true believer in the Bill of Rights, but now I'm a slavish
believer, even ferocious believer in [such concepts as] trial by jury,
presumed innocence."

Salzman said he thought all of these concepts had been settled
in 1789 when the Constitution was adopted, but "then I represented
Stacey and I saw that nothing I believed was true, nothing I had
been taught was legitimate. I see a true verdict in Simi Valley savaged by elected leaders. What happened in his case is that evil men
will triumph when good men do nothing. To me these were just
words before; now they're not just words."

Salzman said he "wasn't truly prepared" for a government prosecution he described as "arrogant and willful, one that believed the end justified the means and everything else be damned. That floored me. I was deficient [as a lawyer] because I wasn't distrustful of government enough."

While he expressed respect for the chief prosecutors as individuals, Salzman said they "truly didn't come to grips with the enormity of their viewpoint—that they had a goal and that no matter what it took to get there, they were going to do it." The government's attitude, he asserted, was, "This is what we're going to do, we're the government, and we can do no wrong."

"I'll never make that mistake again," Salzman concluded. "I'm a lot more distrustful of government than I was before."

The principal courtroom player in putting Koon and Powell in prison was **Barry Kowalski**, the lead prosecutor for the government in the federal criminal trial of the Foothill Four. After the trial, Kowalski returned to his position as a senior trial attorney with the Civil Rights Division of the Justice Department. He says he is considering writing a book about the more publicized trials he has conducted—the Rodney King episode among them.

Kowalski expresses a certain sympathy for the convicted officers, a sentiment he says he has had for almost every policeman or policewoman he has prosecuted, because law enforcement is a tough profession. But, he adds, cops have an added obligation to uphold the law, and therefore he does not believe anything was amiss, either morally or legally, in prosecuting Koon, Powell, Briseno, and Wind.

Kowalski's principal trial attorney from the Los Angeles U.S. Attorney's office, **Steven Clymer,** resigned in 1994 and returned to his alma mater, Cornell University, where he now teaches law. Clymer said Briseno's videotaped testimony was helpful in getting convictions of Koon and Powell, even though Clymer conceded Briseno's testimony at Simi Valley was at least partially "not truthful."[11] He added: "But I don't believe he lied about everything." Clymer said he is "definitely very proud" of the role he played in convicting Koon and Powell.

Former LAPD Chief **Daryl Gates** was a victim of the Rodney King episode, too. But except for damage to his ego and perhaps an occasional twinge of conscience, he has suffered little pain. After charges that he failed to manage affairs properly during the 1992 riots, Gates retired under pressure from the Los Angeles City Council. But he soon launched a new career as a talk-show host, which lasted about eighteen months. He now gives speeches and is a security consultant—his company is called "Chief"—and works with another company engaged in developing interactive videogames. His pension from the city of Los Angeles is more than $100,000 a year.

Gates, you may recall, was the LAPD manager who broadcast a video to his officers directly after the Rodney King episode saying, in effect, that any cop who embarrasses the Los Angeles Police Department as the Foothill Four had done would "rue the day." But today, as one of the victims of the Rodney King episode, Gates has changed his story somewhat.

Now, he said, "I don't think Stacey Koon is guilty of anything except his own bravado. He made himself a principal in this thing. Neither Stacey Koon nor [Laurence] Powell is guilty of violating the civil rights of Rodney King.... Neither one had that intent."[12] Perhaps the officers erred, Gates said. Even so, the reaction by the media, the civil rights community, and the federal government was an "overreaction... that started out to be political and then got worse." Moreover, Gates expressed a belief that he and the department were the real targets. When President Bush made his statement, Gates said, "the gong was sounded and the Civil Rights section of the Justice Department did what they'd been wanting to do for years—and that was step in and get Los Angeles police officers." What made the Rodney King episode different from other civil rights cases, Gates continued, "was the belief by the president of the United States and the belief by others that this [incident] was so political and so necessary that we'd better go ahead with it.

"Every time I think about this... it's such a frightening thing," Gates concluded. "Particularly in Stacey's case. He didn't do anything [wrong]. Maybe he made a supervisory error and then stuck up for his people. But if that's going to cause people to go to prison for as long as he went to prison, we're in trouble in the United States. Deep trouble."

Sergeant Charles Duke was unofficially disciplined in an almost biblical fashion by the Los Angeles Police Department for testifying on behalf of Koon, Powell, Wind, and Briseno at both the Simi Valley and federal criminal trials. He was removed from his position as an unarmed combat and use-of-force instructor at the LAPD training academy and placed in a frontline position on the LAPD's special situation SWAT team that confronts the most dangerous tactical situations. Duke expresses no surprise at the transfer and publicly declines to describe it as departmental reprisal.[13]

Rolando Solano, who on March 3, 1991, rode with Officer Theodore Briseno, has now achieved Patrol III status and qualified as a training officer himself. He says the department has visited no retaliation on him for his support of and testimony for the Foothill Four. Solano says he intends to remain in police work and views Stacey Koon as a model commander. "I think he is a hero," Solano said.[14]

Officer Susan Clemmer, like Solano, provides one of the few bright spots in the entire dreary affair. She met her future husband at a rally to raise money for Laurence Powell's defense. Now a detective in the San Fernando Valley area of LAPD operations, Clemmer said her career goal once was to become an FBI agent. "No more, though," after her experiences with federal prosecutors and the FBI in the Rodney King episode. Nor will she ever again work street patrol—it's too dangerous, not physically but from a political standpoint. "I'll never again react to that scenario where you respond to a call and react to someone needing assistance," she said. "I'll never go back to patrol."[15]

Finally, it should be noted that the **Los Angeles Police Department** has made some reforms to fill the gap in policy that led to the Rodney King affair. But the "reforms" are hardly the stuff of revolutionary change.

For one thing, the LAPD now gives officers "pepper mace," an aerosol spray based on red-hot cayenne pepper and used to subdue violent suspects. The LAPD didn't adopt the pepper mace voluntarily; it did so at the behest of the California legislature, which, after the Rodney King episode, required police officers to adopt tactics to use as an alternative to the PR 24 baton.

Oh, and one other thing:

Remember the "swarm" policy that could have been used on March 3, 1991, to avoid beating Rodney King?

The use-of-force technique that federal prosecutors and prosecution witness Sergeant Mark Conta insisted was available to Koon, Powell, Wind, and Briseno?

The "swarm" technique that could have taken Rodney King into custody more peacefully and avoided violence?

The unused "swarm" procedure that proved the officers acted from malice, since they eschewed it in favor of the PR 24 baton?

In the first week of September 1995, two years and five months after Koon and Powell were convicted, almost two years after they had gone to prison, the Los Angeles Police Department issued a new *Use of Force Handbook*. The manual proudly announced that officers were now authorized, *for the first time*, to use the "swarm" to subdue a combative suspect. The "new" policy was overdue by only four and a half years and at the cost of untold suffering in countless people's lives.

CHRONOLOGY OF MAJOR EVENTS

1991

March 3: Rodney King is arrested after a high-speed chase. The arrest is videotaped from more than one hundred yards away by amateur cameraman George Holliday. The edited version of the tape is first aired on the 10:00 P.M. KTLA-TV news broadcast on March 4. It is picked up immediately by Cable News Network and by the next day has been broadcast worldwide.

March 14: A Los Angeles County grand jury indicts Sergeant Stacey C. Koon, Officers Laurence Powell and Theodore Briseno, and probationary Officer Timothy Wind on state charges of illegally using excessive force to subdue felony evader Rodney King.

March 15: Koon, Powell, Briseno, and Wind are suspended from duty without pay.

1992

February 3: State trial of the four officers begins at Simi Valley in Ventura County.

April 29:
(**3:15 P.M.**) Koon, Briseno, and Wind are found not guilty of all charges. Powell is found not guilty on one charge, but the jury is unable to reach a verdict on one other count.

(**5:00 P.M.**) Los Angeles riots begin, ultimately resulting in at least fifty-three deaths, hundreds more injured, more than seven thousand people arrested, and almost $1 billion in property damage.

April 30: President George Bush announces he has ordered a Justice Department investigation into federal charges of violating Rodney King's civil rights.

August 4: Federal grand jury in Los Angeles returns indictments against the four officers.

1993

February 25: Jury trial in U.S. District Judge John G. Davies's court begins.

April 16: Koon and Powell are found guilty on one charge each of violating Rodney King's civil rights. Briseno and Wind are found not guilty. The verdict is delayed until April 17, to permit Los Angeles and federal officials to prepare for possibility of more disorders. No civil disturbances follow the verdict, which is quickly overshadowed in the media by the FBI raid at Waco on April 19.

August 4: Koon and Powell are sentenced by Judge Davies to thirty months in a federal correctional work camp. They ask to be released on bail during the appellate process. Judge Davies grants the request. Minority and civil rights leaders protest both the sentence and bail as too lenient.

August 27: The Justice Department files an appeal with the Ninth U.S. Circuit Court of Appeals protesting the sentence as too light and asking that bail be revoked. The circuit court agrees. Bail is denied, and the sentence is returned to Judge Davies for imposition of a more severe penalty. Koon and Powell file an appeal of the decision with the U.S. Supreme Court.

October 4: The Supreme Court issues a ruling denying bail to the officers.

October 13: Koon reports to Camp Parks in Dublin, California, in the San Francisco Bay area to begin serving his sentence; Powell had reported the day before.

1994

March 22: First phase of Rodney King's civil suit against the city of Los Angeles begins in Judge Davies's court.

April 19: First phase ends, with the jury awarding King $3.8 million in damages from the city.

April 22: Second phase of King's suit against the officers, seeking at least $15 million in damages, begins in Judge Davies's court.

June 1: Civil trial against the officers ends, with the racially mixed jury awarding King $0 in damages. The jury also finds that King battered Officer Briseno on March 3, 1991, but assesses no damages against King.

1995

January 13: The Ninth U.S. Circuit Court of Appeals formally rejects Koon's and Powell's appeal of its decision to return the sentences to Judge Davies for imposition of a more severe penalty.

April 10: Koon and Powell file a *writ of certiorari* with the U.S. Supreme Court arguing that the Ninth U.S. Circuit Court of

Appeals order to impose tougher sentences violates their rights under the Fourth, Fifth, Sixth, and Fourteenth Amendments to the Constitution.

September 28: The Supreme Court agrees to hear arguments on the issue of whether the order to resentence was in violation of the Constitution.

October 15: Koon is released from the Federal Correctional Work Camp at Sheridan, Oregon, to enter a halfway house and prepare for eventual release on December 14. Powell had been released to a halfway house about two weeks earlier.

November 23: An armed black gang member invades a halfway house in Rubidoux, California, intending to murder Stacey Koon for his involvement in the Rodney King episode. Koon is not there but at home with his family for the holiday. The gunman dies in a shootout with a police SWAT team after killing one hostage, wounding a second, and pistol-whipping a third.

1996

January–June: Time frame established by the Supreme Court for hearing oral arguments on Koon and Powell's appeal and issuing a ruling on whether the sentences should be remanded to Judge Davies for a more harsh punishment and, possibly, an order returning them to prison for an additional seven to eight years.

ABOUT THE AUTHOR

Robert Deitz has been a journalist, editor, and author since 1962. He has worked for newspapers in Kentucky, Washington, D.C., and Texas, and co-authored books on the savings and loan scandal, the oil and gas industry, and, with Stacey C. Koon, *Presumed Guilty: The Tragedy of the Rodney King Affair.* He was a Nieman Fellow at Harvard University in 1971–72 and currently is writing a nonfiction book on violence in America and a Civil War novel about espionage, murder, and John Wilkes Booth. He lives in Dallas with his wife, Sharon.

NOTES

Author's Introduction

1. For the Louisville, Kentucky, *Courier-Journal*, a newspaper long regarded and widely applauded as a voice of liberalism and racial equality in the segregated South.

2. Council on Federated Organizations, a loose association of groups that included the National Association for the Advancement of Colored People (NAACP), CORE, and the Student Non-Violent Coordinating Committee, among others.

Chapter II

1. Telephone interview with the author.

2. Interview with the author.

3. Although she said it, she did not take "full responsibility" for the incident. In fact, she took no responsibility at all. Subordinate FBI officials were mildly disciplined for failures of command judgment, but Attorney General Reno was never even blandly reproved by the president. Neither did she fall upon her sword in penance, as her *mea culpa* would seem to suggest. In fact, the meaningless

assumption of "full responsibility" for a deadly decision that cost more than eighty lives was all she said about possible mistakes concerning Waco until critics began asking embarrassing questions.

4.   And, in fact, this is precisely what occurred. The officers were charged with violating a standard that *did not even exist at the time of the alleged offense, and in fact never did exist until more than two years after their convictions.* This key element will be discussed in more detail later in this book. It is important to note here only because few people took notice of it at the time, although it was obvious to those who were not following a political agenda.

5.   And it's worth observing that the same hypocritical standard was employed by the Justice Department in letting agents off the hook for the deadly raid on a survivalist's cabin at Ruby Ridge in Idaho. How many coincidental events are required to form a pattern of behavior?

6.   Op. cit., author's interview.

7.   Typically, in retelling the incident that led to the trial, the *Times* described Rodney King as simply "a black man who was stopped for speeding." No mention was made of the charge of felony evasion, his resistance to arrest, or the fact that he was drunk, all of which Rodney King admitted under oath on the witness stand.

Chapter III

1.   Or they have won two and a half out of three, if you count the innocent verdicts against Wind and Briseno in federal court as half of the trial.

2.   This incident is discussed in more detail in Koon's book, *Presumed Guilty.* After March 3, 1991, the LAPD investigated every incident in which Stacey Koon had even been mentioned in complaints about police misbehavior, with special attention given to potential implications of racial bias. Despite all efforts, no misconduct could be found. This particular incident, though, is powerful evidence that

Koon is not a racist. Ask yourself this question: In this day of AIDS, would you give mouth-to-mouth resuscitation therapy to anyone, much less a high-risk AIDS carrier like a male prostitute? And if you were a white racist cop, would you administer such treatment to a black male prostitute? The answer is obvious.

3.   And, in fact, one of the disciplinary notations was paradoxically related to the commendation for giving mouth-to-mouth resuscitation to the black male prostitute; department supervisors said the action demonstrated a "lack of common sense."

4.   The same panel heard both cases because the suit originally was filed against the officers *and* the city of Los Angeles. To simplify matters, Judge Davies, who also heard the civil proceedings, "bifurcated," or split, the trial into two segments, with the city trial conducted first and the civil charges against the officers tried afterward.

5.   The *Los Angeles Times*, embarrassed, perhaps, by a decision that contradicted its reporting and editorial commentary on the incident, emphasized not the fact that King was awarded no damages but that the officers had "acted in reckless disregard" of King's constitutional rights.

6.   Koon has another amusing story to tell about the "Cadillac" cigarette-butt sweepers. A new inmate who hadn't yet learned prison jargon was chastised by a prison guard for standing around, hands in pockets, doing nothing productive in a federal work camp. "Go find a Cadillac and get to work," the female guard ordered the new inmate. Koon could not suppress a smile when the new prisoner indignantly protested, "Hey, ma'am, I'm not in here for pimpin'."

7.   Meaning that Koon was the 21,667th officer sworn into service since the LAPD was formed about 1870.

8.   The *Chicago Tribune*, the *Christian Science Monitor*, the *Los Angeles Times*, the *New York Times*, the *Wall Street Journal*, and the *Washington Post*. The InfoTrac system was selected because it indexes only

major articles, thus sifting out smaller items of usually more localized or negligible interest to general readers.

9.   The Magazine Article Summaries FullTEXT retrieval service shows that during this period *Time* published seven articles about Koon; *Newsweek,* five; and *U.S. News & World Report,* three. All were uniformly negative about the officers' conduct. For example, one *Time* article reported that during the arrest on March 3, 1991, Rodney King received "half a dozen blows to the head from Koon alone," although the videotape clearly showed that Koon did no such thing. Although *Time* later retracted the statement, the error reveals the kind of bias, perhaps unconscious bias to be generous, that permeated media reporting of the incident.

10. Some other people with CIM status are organized crime boss John Gotti, imprisoned at a new maximum-security facility in Colorado, and Jeffrey MacDonald, the former U.S. Army Green Beret doctor convicted of murdering his wife and children.

11. Koon jokingly refers to his first few months in prison as an accelerated graduate program in the Jenny Craig weight-loss curriculum.

12. The highest, or most severe, level of punishment is a federal prison, such as the ones at Atlanta and in Colorado.

13. Some inmates are assigned full-time jobs with UNICOR, the BOP-operated business that makes furniture, fixtures, clothing, and other items intended for use by all federal agencies. These jobs can pay $200 a month or more. But they usually are assigned to inmates who have been ordered to pay restitution to the government, and UNICOR takes most of their pay as money due to the government. Koon was not ordered to pay restitution, so he was assigned a menial task. The purpose of a work camp is to work, and every inmate is assigned specific duties.

14. In fact, during a brief telephone conversation with the author, Lerman said he believed the only people who would read

this book were "trailer-park, red-neck white trash," a description so colorful that the author could not resist including it, even if only as an endnote.

15. The suit for payment of attorneys' fees included the police defendants. But, as noted earlier, Judge Davies said that since King did not win his civil suit against the cops, he was not entitled to recover from them any money for attorneys' fees or out-of-pocket expenses. The city, though, was liable since it had lost the suit King filed.

16. The name was even used as a verb form by some young black men. "The police ain't going to Rodney King me," one black youth told a national magazine during the 1992 LA riots.

17. The other passenger, Freddy Helms, was killed in an automobile accident in June 1991.

18. Bryant Allen got a small settlement from the city, about $30,000, but most if not all of it was eaten up by attorney's fees, according to court records.

19. Although it was hardly the first time, which everyone knew.

20. Once on the scene, the deputy chief ordered that Rodney King not be arrested, even though the LAPD at that time required that any suspect accused of spousal abuse be taken into custody. The investigating officer demanded that the deputy chief order him to release Rodney King, since releasing King would violate departmental policies.

21. Prompting one late-night media wit to joke that "the bad news is that Rodney King has been arrested again for drunk driving, and the real bad news is that he has to drive from California to Pennsylvania to stand trial."

22. At this writing, both the Pennsylvania and Alhambra charges are pending.

Chapter IV

1. For Koon's complete account of the arrest of Rodney King, please see his book, *Presumed Guilty: The Tragedy of the Rodney King Affair* (Washington, D.C.: Regnery Gateway, 1992), pp. 17–52.

2. Few people run from cops late at night unless they've been involved in something more serious than speeding, such as robbery, assault, drug possession, and so on. This consideration persuaded Koon and the other officers present that King was not just a simple speeder—which, of course, he was not.

3. One of which was King's physical appearance. He was "buffed out," Koon said, meaning that King apparently had been engaged in an intensive body-building regimen, which many convicts follow in prison.

4. King later was tested for PCP with a urinalysis done at Pacifica Hospital, but the tests were inconclusive because his urine had such a high pH content because of the copious quantities of alcohol he had consumed. So whether he was dusted with PCP that night could be neither proved nor disproved.

5. TASER is an acronym for the whimsically titled "Thomas A. Swift Electric Rifle," named by its manufacturer for the inventive fictional hero of juvenile novels.

6. Koon, *Presumed Guilty*, p. 45.

7. The jail will not accept PCP suspects. Anyone taken into custody with such a diagnosis, as Rodney King was, has to be transferred to LACUSCMC.

8. "U" meaning the pronoun "you," and not "unit," or squad car. Koon sent the message to urge Lieutenant Conmay to come to the scene if Conmay believed a more senior supervisor was necessary.

9. Confidential internal report by Special Agent Jerry D. Delap, dictation dated March 7, 1991, based on interview conducted on March 6, 1991.

10. For a more thorough explanation of the LAPD's use-of-force policies, please see Koon, *Presumed Guilty*, pp. 53–64.

11. *Newsweek*, 9 May 1994, p. 26.

Chapter V

1. This is a personal observation. The author served on a federal grand jury for eighteen months in the early 1980s, and the experience was a jarring exposure to how the grand jury system operates in the real world. In theory, a grand jury is supposed to be a neutral body that examines evidence to determine (1) if a crime has been committed and (2) if so, the likelihood that the crime was committed by a particular person or persons. In practice, a federal grand jury is a prosecutorial tool a U.S. attorney can wield for any reason—including politics.

2. Which is to say when the Bush administration was elected, just in case anyone missed the point.

3. Interview with the author.

4. Judge Davies later ruled that any acts of alleged misconduct would not be allowed into evidence, which was not any real help to Koon's defense since no evidence of serious misdeeds could be uncovered.

5. Which is why Judge Davies refused to allow the "Gorillas in the Mist" radio transmission to be admitted into evidence at the trial.

6. I know this to be a fact, since the notes were the basis of Sergeant Koon's book, *Presumed Guilty*, the preparation of which I assisted. I have read all of the rough notes. "Mandingo" was taken out of context by the *Los Angeles Times* reporter who wrote about it;

the other material was about what Koon had heard other officers say, in contrast with his own and his officers' behavior on March 3, 1991.

7. Interview with the author.

8. So named for the body's chairman, Warren Christopher, who became President Clinton's secretary of state.

9. Although, as noted in Chapter IV, in March and April 1991 portions of Koon's allegedly confidential statements to the Internal Affairs Division of the LAPD were leaked to the media, thus presumably making his statements available to anyone for the price of a newspaper.

10. In cross-examining Koon, prosecutors were able to score valid points by noting that in his book *Presumed Guilty* Koon had described the gang-tackle of Rodney King as a "swarm" within LAPD policy. It was a poor choice of words, for which I must bear some responsibility as co-author of the book. Had either of us been aware of the importance this issue would later take, doubtless we would have been less careless.

11. George P. Fletcher, *With Justice for Some* (Reading, Mass.: Addison Wesley Pub. Co., 1995), pp. 60–61.

12. Briseno did testify at the civil trial in which Rodney King sought damages from the officers and there blunted somewhat his criticism of the use of force employed to subdue King. His attorney, Harland Braun, said the reason he did so was because "at Simi Valley he saw the incident from one particular point of view, and before the federal trial the government had been able to do a stabilized video, which made certain things clearer." Braun said that when Briseno "saw the way it was happening [on the enhanced government video], as opposed to the way he *thought* he saw it was happening at the scene… he could see why Powell would be hitting Rodney King—it gave him another perspective."

13. Or, perhaps more accurately, racial politics.

14. Interview with the author.

15. Maria Esquibel, a juror, is named here because she abandoned her anonymity for newspaper interviews after the trial.

Chapter VI

1. Grimes, you will recall, is now suing King for more than $1 million in unpaid legal bills, according to Grimes.

2. Meaning the offenses for which they had been convicted.

3. Judge Davies did not address the issue of a conspiracy among the officers to cover up the incident, since the government had made no such formal charge in the indictments. Nor did he touch on the issue of racially inspired motivation on the officers' part, since this wasn't part of the government's case, either. But the government had tried mightily to establish such links and apparently failed. Otherwise, Judge Davies would probably have taken these factors into account in determining punishments.

4. Powell and Wind did not testify in accordance with a trial strategy agreed upon by Salzman and their respective attorneys. Briseno did not testify for reasons explained earlier in this chapter.

5. Emphasis is added because the judge's comment appears to distance him from the jury's finding, to the extent possible.

6. Because the alleged offense was ancient history.

7. The state ultimately dropped the unresolved charge, which involved one count on which the Simi Valley jury could not agree, since the federal government was prosecuting the case.

Chapter VII

1. This explanation is admittedly simplistic, but since this book is not a legal treatise the subject will be dealt with in broad lay terms

rather than the more complex, technical definitions used by lawyers.

2. *Green v. United States.*

3. Darlene Ricker. "Double Jeopardy: Did the Rodney King Trial Violate Double Jeopardy?" *American Bar Association Journal,* August 1993, pp. 66–71.

4. Raising once again the question: Why didn't the federal government prosecute first, if federal charges were more appropriate from the outset?

5. If one argues that Rodney King was in custody when the alleged offense occurred, then it follows that David Koresh and his followers were also in custody when the FBI raided the Branch Davidian compound near Waco. The arguments are as parallel as they are false.

6. *Los Angeles Daily Journal,* 15 April 1993, p. 6.

7. Which, as noted earlier, had also been leaked to newspapers, which printed excerpts from the testimony, thus further contaminating the evidence.

8. This is not to say Judge Fitzgerald was sympathetic to the officers, or that he would buck the Justice Department's intention to inflict the most severe punishments possible on Koon and Powell. He said any "misconduct [by the government] was partially invited, isolated and of limited severity." All of that is true, especially the part about "limited severity," considering what the Justice Department had done and was still trying to do to the officers.

9. Except when Rodney King's offenses are at issue. Then the judicial systems turn a blind eye.

10. Although the Court may consider it as part of the appeal on the resentencing issue; Koon's lawyers argue that after having served

the full sentence originally imposed, an additional term in prison would constitute being "twice put in jeopardy of life or limb."

Chapter VIII

1.   Interview with the author.

2.   In a letter to Judge Davies.

3.   Interview with the author.

4.   *American Police Beat,* October 1995, p. 36.

5.   Cited by *American Police Beat,* January/February 1995, pp. 6–7.

6.   As matters turned out, Ford was not charged. The seventeen-year-old girl was plea-bargained out and charged with unlawfully discharging a firearm within the city limits, rather than for attempted murder of a police officer.

7.   Which was one of the reasons why King said he wanted to return to Hansen Dam Recreational Park on the night of March 3, 1991—because his father had taken him fishing there many years before. This testimony conflicted with that provided by one of King's companions that night, Bryant Allen, who said they were either looking for women or seeking to buy more beer.

8.   Interview with the author.

9.   Interview with the author.

10. Interview with the author.

11. Interview with the author.

12. Interview with the author.

13. Interview with the author.

14. Interview with the author.

15. Interview with the author.

INDEX